I wish to thank Marie de L. Welch
and the people of Kerry

THE ORGY

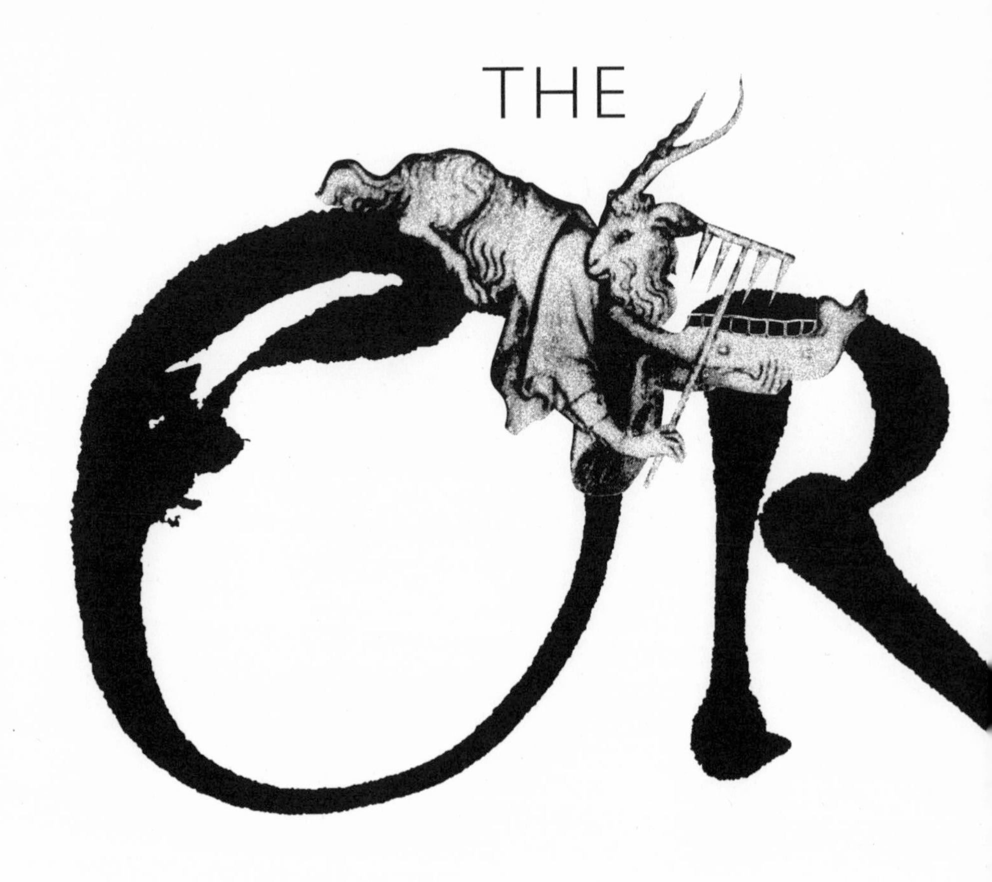

An Irish Journey of Passion and Transformation

MURIEL RUKEYSER

With a Preface by Sharon Olds

PARIS
PRESS
ASHFIELD
MASSACHUSETTS
1997

 For information address Paris Press, Inc., P.O. Box 578, Ashfield, MA 01330; e-mail: parispr@crocker.com; www.westmass.com/Paris-Press.

Paris Press gratefully acknowledges the generous assistance of those individuals, foundations, and organizations who support our work.

The painting on the cover, "Les Amants au ciel rouge" (1950), oil on canvas, 25⁵/₈ x 26¹/₈ in., by Marc Chagall, is reprinted by permission of the San Francisco Museum of Modern Art, gift of Wilbur D. May.

Book design by Ivan Holmes.
Jacket lettering by Judythe Sieck.

Library of Congress Cataloging-in-Publication Data

Rukeyser, Muriel, 1913-1980
The orgy : an Irish journey of passion and transformation / by Muriel Rukeyser ; with a new preface by Sharon Olds. — 1st Paris Press ed.
p. cm.
ISBN 0-9638183-2-5 (alk. paper)
I. Title.
PS3535.U4068 1997
813'.52—dc21 97-23632
CIP

1st ed. New York: Coward-McCann, Inc., © 1965 Muriel Rukeyser
Reprinted New York: Pocket Books, © 1966 Muriel Rukeyser
First Paris Press Edition, 1997

0 9 8 7 6 5 4 3 2 1

Printed in the United States of America

CONTENTS

PUBLISHER'S NOTE

THOSE WHO have traveled know the experience of extended time and sharpened perception. Muriel Rukeyser's account of Puck Fair captures just that state of consciousness. Set in County Kerry, Ireland, at the last existing pagan festival of the goat, *The Orgy* evokes this great American poet's journey of sensual and psychological transformation.

The Orgy is Rukeyser's exemplar of feeling fully—it is a sensual feast. Originally published by Coward-McCann in 1965 and reprinted in 1966 by Pocket Books, *The Orgy* is deeply controversial, like all of Rukeyser's ground-breaking works. Many critics have applauded this "luminous" account, while others have objected to Rukeyser's personal unveilings, her characteristic mixing of genres, and the daring revelations about female eroticism, male sexuality, hatred, isolation, psychoanalytic theory, and Irish culture.

Only a few of Rukeyser's admirers have read this book. It has been out of print in the U.S. since 1967, and nearly impossible to find—even for the most dedicated sleuths. *The Orgy* follows Paris Press's publication of *The Life of Poetry*, and it illustrates nearly everything that the poet discusses in her *tour de force* exploration of American culture: We must feel fully in order to live fully. We must challenge ourselves to break through the safety of limited consciousness and constricted experience. We must open ourselves to all our senses, to memory and association, and to "taboo." "The orgy," says Muriel Rukeyser, "is experience."

Muriel Rukeyser's work always refuses simple categorizing. In *The Orgy*, as in her poems, her essays, plays, and her biographies, she breaks the boundaries between prose and poetry, autobiography and fiction, the imagined and the real, the present and the past. *The Orgy* recounts Rukeyser's travels in County Kerry as she attended Puck Fair in 1958 on a research project for the documentary filmmaker, Paul Rotha. Due to issues of privacy as well as political concerns in Ireland and the United States, *The Orgy* was first published as a novel. Happily, the political climate has changed, and Paris Press presents *The Orgy* to you as it was intended by the author—a memoir.

In this new edition, we have used the original 1965 Coward-McCann edition, along with the revised text of the 1966 Pocket Books edition. We have corrected certain names, amended some inaccuracies, and omitted the Notes, which Rukeyser included in the earlier editions as documentation of Puck Fair. Her account of the event now stands on its own, based on her experience in Killorglin.

We offer our heartfelt appreciation to the many individuals and organizations who made the publication of *The Orgy* possible: The Massachusetts Cultural Council, The Sonia Raiziss Giop Charitable Foundation, CLMP, The Lydia B. Stokes Trust, Patricia McCambridge, Adrian Oktenberg, Rebecca Bell, Anne Goldstein, Carol Potter, Sawnie Morris, Cel Noll, Bruno Bouissiere, Julie Van Pelt, Judythe Sieck, and Ivan Holmes. Special thanks always to William L. Rukeyser.

—Jan Freeman

PREFACE

THIS IS an extraordinary book, built on an extraordinary act: an American woman goes alone, in 1958, to an Irish festival of drink and sex. When her close chance companions leave the festivities at night, she stays on, embracing, kissing—a single mother, thirties radical, Jewish, in a small Irish market-town.

The Orgy is the record of a quest—for an understanding of the relative powers, in us, of destruction and creation. It is the story of a search less for sexual experience than for knowledge of the meaning of sexual experience.

The quest in *The Orgy* is undertaken in patriarchy, under the maleness of the goat on the tower. It is a quest for the speaker's own nature, and it is a search for a male principle, or for knowledge of the male, or knowledge of the speaker's father.

The Orgy is a search for the meaning of family. It is a tale of disconnecting and joining with. It is a prayer about how to shape one's life. It is about blood lines and sympathy lines, about war and sexual war, about peace and the sexual dance.

The Orgy records a quest for the meaning of nationality, and history, and religion. It is a search for transformation and love.

It is an odyssey written at a crossroads. It is a tale in which issues of loneliness, autonomy, oppression, sexual identity, prejudice, and sexual preference lie on or just under the surface.

This book is the expression of an unafraid sense of the human—Muriel Rukeyser has the stomach for it, the tolerance and pleasure-in-truth. She wants, in one short book, to answer basic questions about war and sex, female and male, American and Irish, Jew and Gentile, artist and analyst, joy and depression, the fear of and the lust for people, the short life and the long art, the ordinary and sublime, shit and the sacred individual, happenstance and cause, purposiveness and stymied momentum.

The Orgy has layers, and secrets. It refers to things it's not going to tell, and tells us it's not going to tell. It is a message in a bottle—a brilliant packet of messages in a far-traveled bottle.

—Sharon Olds

THE ORGY

The goat is real; Puck Fair is real; the orgy is real. All the characters and the acts of this book, however, are—of course—a free fantasy on the event.

GATHERING DAY

1

I CAME to that coast.—

But what kind of a book is this? That place I did not know, the wildness turned loose in the crowd looking up to the goat on his blue tower, that penitential landscape with its sea and its praying crags, that other mythical beast—an English analyst practicing in Ireland—people I did not know, the invisible castle in the shape of a tree, all things roused up among the music, the lights and the filth of cattle. I don't know what it is saying to me.

I came to the coast of Kerry.—

How could I ever say how I got there, what sense does it make to tell what those lies really were? The police sergeant at the barracks saying to me, "You're welcome if you don't mind our lying." And I said, "I know your kind of lying, I know it in myself. As far as I can make out, people say one thing in the beginning. Then they say something that completely contradicts the first. The truth turns out to be the first thing, but with an entirely different meaning." He told me I was welcome to anything there was. But what have all the gypsies lined up in their painted carts—the tinkers—across the river to do with that, the kicking of the tinker woman?

I can hear the bartender's shoe knocking on bone when he kicked her. And what happened then? Or the curious banal thing that Nicholas finally said to me, that I could never set down in writing. But if I tell that story, these are its pieces. They move together, flowing and racing with that sea in the channel, blue and green, with the green green land and its dark mountains lifted over, and the offshore island ahead.

That coast stretches out in two legs, and between them the bay over which Lindbergh flew, yelling to the fishing boat. The two legs of land push deep out into the Atlantic, from the mountains—The Paps, and then the higher ones, and the greatest of all, The Left-handed Reaping Hook, Carrantuohill—out past its feudal landscapes, dominated by three huge buildings: the church with the cross cut gold into its side, the ruined castle, and the turf generator. Out past its tawny mile-long beaches that strike out into the bay, now purple barred, a donkey watching while a man sleeps in the dune, under sword-grass. Far out to where I stand in slashing rain, although behind me the sun is on a whole slope of the mountain. The island channel before me. And back there, where those two legs meet; at the crotch there is the town where the goat will stand on his tower, the most handsome goat in the world. Crowned, elevated, he will be tied there for three days and nights. He is king.

Everywhere, from all over the country, people are converging on the little town. In the farm contracts, they sign for a year, with three days off for Puck. I don't know the town. I had a glimpse of it on my way here. "An uninviting little market town," the guidebook says.

What am I doing here? I have flown halfway across the world. It turns out that I am going by myself to an orgy.

The rain is painting the stones of the dock. Everyone has got off the train that has come slowly all day across Ireland to the end of land. We wait for the open boat, a long dory with an engine, pushing wave after wave. The coughing of the engine comes near.

A man of kindness and endless curiosity about New York has taken my bag. The rain paints the stones black and his shoes bright brown. He smiles, broken-toothed and very friendly. The boat is waiting for a smaller boat to be loaded with oil drums, Shell, and large cartons of vegetables and ice cream. Now we go down the water-steps— "Mind them, they're slippy"—and over the rocking gunwale to the wet seats along it, across it, and beyond the coughing, panting engine in its house of wood.... There are about twenty-five of us crossing to the island.

As the boat swings clear of the stone dock, and begins its long slant into the current, I see the ship anchored in mid-channel, and the sailors crowded along the near rail of the trawler as we come close. The black, rounded ship rides high on the water. There seem to be many vermilion snakes climbing her sides, rising and rippling up out of the water in their energy of fire. "Spanish boat," says the man beside me. "They come here all the time, put into channel if a sailor needs doctoring, or to take on water." Now we are very close; the forms of snakes have changed to the peeling of paint, broken in ripples down to the red lead. The Spanish sailors looked down to us; they called across the channel waves. We called and waved; I called; and our boat changed course, and fast, with the current, crossed over to the island. The rain fell. Behind us, the sun had moved to another mountain. The treeless evening in this country. Alone, lit up by newness, ignorant.

2

"DIRTY, the Spanish boats," said Owen Cross. He was proud of his inn. "I wish they'd go." He wished I had seen the new lifeboat instead. "It's down there, drawn up in its shed beside the pier. The latest, just like the one they have in Cornwall. Radar, tinned soup, everything." They had had a naming ceremony for the lifeboat, with the Spanish ambassador officiating. "A charming fellow," said Owen Cross. "All we needed was ticker tape. I have nothing against the Spanish, you understand."

I thought: I have something against the Spanish. For the Spanish, too, in their bravery and defeat. "I should think you could get all the tape in the world. This is where the Atlantic cable comes up out of the sea."

"You know that, do you?" He is a handsome brown, beak-nosed man with black eyes. He glittered at me. "Paul wrote me about you, of course; but you'll forgive me if I can't see why you want to go to Puck Fair." Behind the surface of the innkeeper there was a many-edged quartz calculation; now he waited for me.

He reminded me of Jonah, the turn of neck and shoulder as he waited saying so much about his body and the quality of attention. But many men and almost all things reminded me of Jonah these days. It was in the tension. He hoped he would not be disappointed in what he was about to hear, Jonah did; Owen Cross was fairly sure he would be disappointed, and I could see that his back was braced against it. I felt the importance in his braced back and neck. I talked to him.

The day rolled open. We sat in leather chairs, our knees near, in the library of the island inn. It was late, and the other guests had gone upstairs, all but a core at the bar drinking and playing pocket billiards. I knew that Scattery and Mary Antrim would be there, the priest and the couple from Liverpool and the motorcycle racer. We had talked at dinner and before dinner.

Now I went back to morning, back to two in the morning, landing at Dublin Airport, and what the guard had said about sending a ship to the moon. I went back to the ride through Dublin in dark night, struck with street-light so that the Post Office stood clear, mythic in all the poems and history. The night at Dun Laoghaire, and the morning train. The lion-faced woman with the woman who had heard just now that her son had been killed in Putney; the care of her, her friends, the tea. The white horse racing across the long field away from the train, the couples taking in the hay, the green stations; the grief-stricken children with their father leaving; suffering of poverty, ragged along the roads, standing at exposed train-crossings, their wrists thrust out, their big hands red; his rifle down to help his 86-year-old mother, whose turkeys the fox was getting; the girl trained in Dublin as a stenographer, with no typewriters in Ireland; the glimpse of Killorglin, where the goat would be crowned; and if this, whatever it was, emerged from these bodies, this suffering known and unknown to me, a day like this reaching into this landscape. If this were goat-haunted as I had been goat-haunted the last month. I wanted to be open to it; I had ignorance; something was coming that spoke for what had spoken to me today. I did not know what that was.

Owen looked into my face. "I'll drive you to Killorglin tomorrow. You'll meet my friends in the town, and we'll find a place for you to stay the three days. A place nearer than here. You'll want to see the whole thing."

"You're going to it, aren't you?"

"Me going to Puck?" He laughed. "Not any more. I could tell you about the black market during the war, and the fighting of women, the brawling. Did you ever see *Shane*?" He looked at me. "Paul was right in sending you. But he should be here himself too."

This is the way Paul Rotha had told me about it.

There is a town on the west coast of Ireland, he said. It looks like a drab little Victorian town. And is, except for three days of the year, in August. Now a month before that the men have gone out into the mountains—MacGillycuddy's Reeks, the highest in Ireland, and you must say Macklicoody—and they have found and caught the handsomest goat in the world. They catch him and for a month they treat him better than any goat has ever been treated. All this time people from all over are converging on the town—all over Kerry, of course, all over the country, and from Persia, they say, and Spain, and Europe, and cops in New York save up all year to go to Puck. The night before the Fair, all the little shops around the square, that sell all the things little shops sell—they close, and in the morning when they open, each one is a pub. The goat is crowned king—they say the tinkers choose their king there, too, but that of course is done in secret. The town is wide open, they say. It's the last of the goat festivals: Greece, Spain, Scotland, England—the last.

I was making a tinker film in Cork, he said. That's how I know Owen Cross. He was running a hotel there, those years, and he's in my film—for just a minute, I'll do better next time. I had a call out for extras, I needed a man for the farmer. They brought this man Art, I knew the minute I saw him. He played the farmer well. During the break one day, he told me about Puck Fair. Art Murnahan his name was, he'd been collecting material about it, he said. Last month I had a letter from his daughter. He had just died, she wrote, and left me the material. There isn't much, really. The thing would be for you to go and look at it. But you couldn't do that on your own; I'd meet you and make notes for shooting, and arrange for camera positions and a studio to work from, and make the film the following August.

He handed me the envelope with Art Murnahan's notes and clippings.

3

PERHAPS Paul will still arrive in time, although I very much doubt it. He sat there, in New York, telling me that there was such a town, that there was such a goat, and for that matter that there was such a kingdom as Kerry. But I doubt that he will come in, by plane or train. He sat there, russet-color, smoking the cigar he loves. Let him bring his cameras, I am not going to be an American woman carrying a camera. I have a small blue notebook that will fit in my pocket, or in a pocket of my bag.

Killorglin from the train: yellow houses, and the Ferris wheel up. The river I longed for all last summer in the city, many-flowing, braided water, one fisherman trying his cast as the train passes, swans.

The sense of a vast goat running the tops of the Reeks.

Valentia Island and the Spanish boat. Palm tree clacking outside my window. Lights of the ship at night, a clear constellation after rain. The squared-off mass of the breakwater piers, and, in the left corner, the square gray clock-tower with a window in each wall, the stones of the corners large and uneven all the way up the wall, and then the little endearing cupola, a stopped clock in each of the faces; posted on the near wall, a ferry schedule that has nothing to do with the fact. The ferry goes over when it suits the ferryman. He charges what suits him. I heard the Liverpool people grumble; he grinned at me and said, "A shilling when you go back over." Little orange rowboat. Rocky, cloudy mountains behind.

The woman at the desk of the inn, and the slow cherishing look at Owen Cross. To me she said, I can't recommend any place for lunch in Killorglin, and Are you Catholic? O, most everybody is Catholic in Killorglin.

Mary Antrim, sunburned bright pink. Belfast, giggling, on holiday south—Are you... Have you heard of Rudolf Steiner? In the dining room with its separate tables, I am assigned to her. It's our Auntie Mary, said Owen Cross. You'll find things to talk about. She works as private secretary for the Donn & Galty—big shipbuilding firm. Does she really want to talk about the "etheric body" of plants that heal themselves?

The Liverpool people, in the bay window before dinner. She has relaxed from the mild battering of the channel crossing, but the openness, the stillness, makes her remember the war. The stray black kitten that the inn adopted wreathes about her leg, and

Captain, the inn dog, looks up at us, his head cocked at the angle of Cross's head as he waited for my answer. In Liverpool, during the war, there were the raids, yes, and there were the closed buses always passing. You did not know, the living or the dead. Gibraltar, and the queen went—our young queen, Elizabeth. The woman paused, her blue eyes pausing. My brother went out, she said, first France, then Dunkirk. And then out again, this time to Japan, a prisoner camp at once. Back? Yes, but he was like an old man.

And the priest, starting to tell me of the saving of planeloads on their way to Lourdes this summer. Engine failure, he begins—and breaks off. Are you Catholic, may I ask?

Or the priest on the train, with his rifle, Father Peter Lynch with his fine-cut profile, the scar running down his jaw, his lecture about the Skelligs, the crags beyond this island. Skellig Michael—high places named for Michael, Michael's Mount, Mont St. Michel. He lectures on the Skelligs, he tells me, and has slides. He takes a check for an article out of his wallet, three pounds from the Bank na Eireann. All those high places, he says. Up there, near Christ's Saddle, you'll find six beehive cells, a well, a place for rainwater. There, he says, pointing out the window of the train, another ruined castle of the McCarthys. The chocolate fields of turf, laid open by the cutters. The turf lying out and not gathered, the priest said. The hay rotting in the rains.

There is a Spanish sailor hurt, in the hospital on Valentia.

4

I DREAMED that night of Jonah, as he was on our last night before I came to Ireland. We drove up to the restaurant outside of the city, on the river, the nearest place right on the river—then in the dream his face changed to Otto's killed so long ago in Spain. His face as soft as rock under clear water, and my face near

his, under the clear wave with sun ripples on us, ar
brush that went over the drowned faces, brushing,
the features were obliterated.

5

EVERYTHING that is on the island is brought here by boat—food, sheep, any car that comes here, and any gas for it. Owen Cross longs for a tourist island. It has great fishing, he says, it is beautiful, restful, away. If we had a bridge linking us to the mainland, he says—that's what I work for.

"Finish your breakfast?" he asks. "How do you like our bacon?" And I praise it. "I'm going to phone my friend Katy Evans at Glenbeigh," he tells me, at the phone. "Our party's gone off to the Skelligs, the lunches are all packed for the picnickers—hi, here she is! Katy!" He turned to me as he hung up. "As I feared," he said. "She's got every room taken. It's Puck. But we'll go along anyway. That's a resourceful woman. When can you be ready? I can leave the minute lunch is over."

Standing in the bay window of the inn, I could see to the foot of carpeted stairs; the guests came out of the dining room by ones and twos. Most of them had taken their lunches out to the Skelligs or to the strands, down a way to Behy or over to Balinskelligs. The pink-faced secretary was playing with the kitten, tying himself in black knots around her soft wrist, mewing and purring as though he made no difference between them.

"He's a foundling; they took him in," she said, and looked straight up at me. She made a great knot of pink and the orange of her summer dress, with the small black knot about her hand, purring. "Are you still of a mind to go to Puck Fair?" she asked. I told her I was. The strong sense of a bad smell left a print on her face, in the middle of the big pink-and-orange knot. "You won't like it," she said. "It's so materialistic. It's all about drinking."

6

OWEN CROSS stood very straight in the ferry, talking to the ferryman with the lined face and the peakless cap; very Spanish face, dark lines in the sun, and behind him two new Spanish boats, the *Urbasa* from Vigo and the *Udala* from Vigo. The sailors called out from the rail, still out of hearing across the waves, deep color in the channel struck across with bars of light so brilliant that one saw them only as intermittences. You can get some grand brandy cheap, said a man behind us. They have something wrong with the propeller of one of them, said another. Long snakes of light under the ship. "*Mira!*" came a call, and a long gust of singing as we passed. One of the sailors was eating shrimp, raw, on bread, the shrimp whiskers sticking from his mouth as the ferryboat sailed under. They want to *bailar*, a girl said, turning her head and never losing her steady look, the clear column of her neck with its white ridge of muscle taut, her shawl flung back as she stared.

We drove down the road to the highway in Owen's car, parked on the stones of the quay. The cattle pulled away as we reached them; they stood black and short against the wild red of a hedge that went as far as did the road, the hanging reds and pinks and blue-red of fuchsia growing wild. "That's our plant," said Owen, "the tears of Kerry, the blood of Kerry, the curse of Kerry."

It grew fuller and wilder than the reds I remembered from Carmel, that other coast of memory, where there it hung in the gardens, hanging from chains, spilling over pots, red-orange beneath the sexual bells of red, leaning over the edges of urns and among the tiles, and down the white walls. Here it flashed by wild, generous, run to miles of reds. We turned at the main road, passed the shell of the McCarthy castle and in a minute were past the garage and hospital and into the main square of Cahirciveen, past a green house and a lime-green house.

"I think it only right to tell you that I got cold feet after we talked last night," he said, driving off the track. "It's all very well to make friends and drink Irish, and," he turned toward me, not bending at the waist, in a stiff attractive courtly turn, "I could change the fortunes of Valentia Island if you could help me find a rich American wife—but," he looked sharp into my face, "that doesn't mean that an American should go to Puck Fair."

The car stopped in the grass beside the road. We looked up at the walls of a small fortress. The day jolted; what was it? the walls, the building were of the wrong shape, and the criminal sense of wrongness began to seep through. What was it? the building looked like old movies I had seen. Turbans, begging bowls, brave fighting Indians, lancers, Pathan women; the long jagged ridges of the Khyber Pass, flickering in film, rose up. "The Khyber Pass," I said. "Why should that rise up here?"

Owen threw back his head, and howled one acrid laugh. "You've hit it," he said. "This was designed for the Bader—India, right—and there was one designed for here; they got mixed up on the drawing-board, like twins in the play, and there's a fine fort somewhere in the north of Pakistan right now. You see what can happen when people come in here. . . ."

"Knowing nothing at all," I said as he drove back to the road, and turned left again. "In ignorance."

Well, they had worse than ignorance, he said, and was silent. I knew the other name for this country—Iveragh, this coast, these long legs of peninsula, Bloody Iveragh. High before us, cutting off the sea, the powerful great hill, rounded, bare, struck at my sight. The long valley with its church, its attempt at making power that was visible in the turf generator, the broken castle—they were absorbed as light was absorbed in this height that blocked off everything else. And this? I asked him; he told me, Knocknadober.

We went on, Owen talking again about Puck Fair; no, I won't go near it, he said, I know it well and too well. But I could tell you stories, and you should know all of them, if you're really going through this: the black market as it was during the war, and the way the bartenders see it, the way the boys called in from here see it. I'll tell you, he said, it's all hatred and dreariness; do you remember a movie, *Shane*? You do? The fighting that went all through that? long, slow, slugging fighting, breaking everything it passes through? That is how it is at Puck.

7

WE DROVE on; the road had risen up and wound along the cliffs, high over the green and purple waters of Dingle Bay, reaching down to Valentia on one leg, and down the other to the old battles and the country of the poets. We came to a pub at the curve of the road, and Owen suggested we stop. I wanted a bathroom, and said so. He hooted. I suppose you'd like a bath! he crowed. What is the matter with Americans, that they can't say toilet? That's it, isn't it? You know, he said confidingly, I've heard an American say *powder room*! In the pub, three men were talking about Ronny Delaney and the coming football game. I asked the barmaid where the toilet was; she beamed as if I'd asked the question that was the opening key. We've a brand-new one, she said, just put in. Out that door and around the back. Only here, she said, a moment and I'll have it. She was drawing water and filling a bucket. She gave me the bucket. It's a beautiful toilet, she said. The water will soon be connected.

8

COMING to the Inn at Glenbeigh, Owen found the innkeeper, a woman who greeted him, crying out and laughing and bringing us into the bar for an Irish coffee for the American, Katy Evans her name was, and there was not a room anywhere and she was short-handed; all the rooms reserved weeks ago for this week—no, nothing to do with the Fair, these guests are here for the fishing mostly, and the golf, but of course she was short-handed and all the girls were going to Killorglin, she gives them a pound and asks no questions. She turned on me: I hate visitors to see it, she said. Anyway, she said, everything in Ireland looks shabby and dirty after America. Everything looks very real to me, I thought, looking through the window at the people in her garden, and the heads of three men on bicycles behind them in the road; and I said so.

She knows she's ignorant, said Owen. That's a change, isn't it, Katy?

I'd like to use my ignorance.

They looked at me. Well, said Katy Evans, I don't have a thing. But you'll be heading back, will you, after a look at Killorglin? Then stop here on your way to the ferry, and have a cup of tea or something with me.

9

HE TOOK me around Killorglin. A little, empty town, with yellow and cream-color houses, and a few posters the only signs of anything about to happen. I met O. R. Connery, who had written the official pamphlet of the Fair, and stood happily in the doorway of O'Sullivan's bar as Grania O'Sullivan, blonde and easy-talking, told about him; to Regan, the butcher, who offered me a place to watch and rest; and Peter and Noreen at Cahill's, who invited me to wash glasses there the next night, and offered me a spell at a bed for my work; to Lenihan's garage, across the river where one fisherman stood, making his casts, the garage facing the road to Killarney. Now let's go to the barracks, said Owen. And if you should feel like giving them a bottle of Power's—

We bought the bottle, with its gold belt, and went to the corner of the little square. In the middle of it, they were putting up the tower; blue wooden, made of two-by-fours painted blue and knocked together, with a platform on the first floor, an open floor for the second story, and an arrangement of a few boards for the top, with four poles stretching up beyond the top, from the corners of the rickety structure. Two men in shirtsleeves were hammering at the base; a small child peered under, and then bent and squirmed in until he disappeared. One of the men whistled; as we went into the barracks, the child emerged grinning.

In the barracks, two policemen—the Garda—sat in wooden chairs, their caps back, and one said that Sergeant Nolan was not in. Owen Cross asked that he be sent for, and gave his name and mine. The policemen went out of the door; we could hear him on the stairs, and in a minute he came down, footsteps followed by footsteps. The Sergeant came in. It was lovely to see how these people—Mrs. Evans, the butcher, the writer, all—looked at Owen Cross. I gave the bottle to Sergeant Nolan. He was pleased; he took it out of its bag, and set it on the high police desk. This is Guard Tobin, and this is Guard Looby, he said. They touched their caps at me, and looked at the bottle. And you have no place to stay during the time? the Sergeant asked me. Owen told him about Mrs. Evans. Is there anything here? he asked. Well, you know, Mr. Cross, said the Sergeant. There's only the Railway Hotel; and as for that, they're four and six men now in every room in town. You know how it is in Puck? he said, ma'am? What have they told you about it?

I knew there were three days: Gathering Day, the Day of the Fair, and Scattering Day—and isn't that the day of the children?

Sergeant Nolan grinned at the room in an amused way that would allow tolerance. O, he said, that's just a lie that they tell tourists. No, there's nothing about children.

He was telling Owen about his children, upstairs, and how he meant to keep them upstairs while Puck was going on.

I was ten years back, on the north of Vancouver Island with

my small son, not yet two years old; on the track of Franz Boas, I was, and one of his informants had just told me why they liked him—we liked Boas, she said—you know why? and told me something I could get from no book in the world. We liked him because he was on time for meals. I looked out to where my little son was sitting on a huge cedar log with two little Kwakiutl boys, twins, and my son was showing them his "old friend car"—a red metal car, the one toy he had brought. Perhaps it was battered and more silver than red, where the paint had worn; he had lost it that morning, and the twins had helped him find it in the long pale grass. The informant said to me, It is good that you brought your child with you; you know, none of these white scientists bring any family with them . . . no children, nothing; they just appear here, one white man, another white man, asking us silly questions and mispronouncing. You know what our chief amusement in the summer at Port Hardy is? Telling lies to white scientists.

I thought of what I had seen in the train, and of my son and the men and women I loved. I know your lying, I said to Sergeant Nolan. I know it here and I know it in myself. I think your people say one thing, and then they say another thing, but they are acting out the truth all along, you have only to look at them and you will see the truth. He looked at me—Anything we can do for you, we'll be glad to.

Well—said Owen, is it all right then if she wants to watch from your upstairs window? She's more than welcome, said Sergeant Nolan, come up and meet Mrs. Nolan now.

10

ON THE way back, we stopped at the Post Office. Mr. Connery was in the phone booth, speaking to Dublin—"He's phoning in the story to the Dublin *Times*," said the postmaster, and gave me the letter that was waiting for me. I could hear Mr.

Connery saying "KING PUCK—K for Kerry, I for Ireland, N for Nolan, G for Germany; P for Poland, U for Una, C for Church, K—" as I went out, the blue letter from Paul in my hand. I sat in the car and read it while Owen waited. I handed the letter to him.

It isn't as if he didn't want to come, Owen said at last. You can see that in every line. As I see it—maybe distortedly—he writes, it is just impossible; and that about "black obligations." Well, said Owen, let's see what Katy has cooked up.

Katy Evans came out of her kitchen. I've put you in the staff sitting room, dear, she said with her arm around me. The bed's made, and you can have a key to the side door, whenever you come in; there'll be a fire waiting for you, and a thermos of tea. You just go on back to Valentia, Owen; she'll come back to you after Puck.

11

AT DINNER, the dining room of the Inn at Glenbeigh. Patrick Kirwan, making movies at Bray. The formal couple, bent over a post card, holding themselves admirably; both hermaphrodites? He says: Wo reise er denn? And she, in one uninflected word: NachTinternAbbey. And the English family, rose-colored mother, two young children, and her father. You can hardly hear them, except when she says, lilting upward, You *did*? and downward, Nice change.... The little boy asks suddenly, How tall was King Charles? And his grandfather asks why. The boy has been taught that it was one yard from King Charles' nose to his fingertips. The grandfather doesn't know about that; the king must have been a very tall man; no, he says, I didn't know him at all, but I *have* seen King Edward VII—a *most* unpleasant fellow; no neck at all, talked like this; he does something in his throat that sounds like a turkey farm, half a mile away, at dusk. But, he adds, his brother was charming.

12

OUTSIDE my sitting room, the garden. Red, lavender-pink, deep blue flowers in the dusk approaching each other in color; high on their stalks as I sit beneath them in this cool and sunken room. One palm tree there, as one palm tree stands below my window on Valentia Island. Gulls high in the air, from their cries high enough to be flashing in the last light. Light high over the shore, surf incandescent at the foot of the cliffs, sloping up the long beach just beyond, and up the beach that almost meets it, jutting out from the other side of the Bay. Voices beyond the door, guests looking at the things for sale on the Inn counter: Waterford glass, all its cuts flashing; little toy leather currachs with their oars shipped neatly, models from the Blaskets out past Dingle; and, in a curious souvenir of methods, laminated into plastic on a little base, a postage stamp, the ha'penny green of a monk at a table reading a great book, sitting in the sweeping green curve of the Gaelic "e" for *Eire*—and on the other side, painted on the reverse of the stamp, a scene of dark powerful mountains, one humped large like Knocknadober, and the black islands lying in the Bay between mountains and me. I hear the tourist voices just past my glass and curtained door.

13

SOUND of rain in the garden. Waking in the dark, a long shiver of cool and wet garden blown in past the French door blown open. The first long diving into sleep; remembering the first word I ever heard in Ireland: "Mich'l!" and the guard looking up at the moon. By God, said the priest, a miracle already! And the guard, when everyone had gone, they say they'll be going to the moon. It's half now. What will they be going when it's dark? The long night of love before I took the plane; and the quick flight, halfway around the world, the endless hour when the engine failed and the woman across the aisle went into convulsions (the young monkey shaking the grapevines in the garden), and hanging on, my hanging on to the fact that what I was doing was for the sake of being practical finally, that this break of time with all I loved, for the sake of all I loved, was not simply fleeing halfway around the world to go to an orgy.

14

THE FACE of the streaked woman on the train, Bridey, whose son was killed yesterday, in Putney, in a motorbike accident. The white animals of Ireland, a horse running from the scream of the train; sheep, with great witty slashes of paint on their bottoms, red, blue, like laughter, scattering up the hillsides. The yellow houses of Killorglin. The station, with its kerosene light, green how I love you green, waving at the stations, *as* I love you green, wrapping the salmon, green branch, the green sleeves of the ragged children crying for their father. Their Daddy, their Da, gone off by train. The red-lead and black fishing boat, seen in channel, seen from my window between snowball bushes. "Are you Catholic, may I ask?" And Father Peter, with his rifle on his knees, telling me about the man who went to the cart, and asked the man lying under it where someone was. The man lying on his back in the grass said I don't know where he is. Why don't you try the woman upstairs?

15

GREAT cities flash through my night like the white horse through the gap in the fence. Streams reach their whiteness, the sheep-starred mountainsides. And the great mountains turn the coast of the heart. Crowned powers in these mountains, a goat running the mountaintops.

16

LAUGH of a woman in the wet flowers, the wet black road outside, the wetness of the sky, of all things. Deep sleep.

Slept late; woke when one of the inn-girls burst in, remembered I was sleeping there, and left. Slept again; sun in the garden where it rained all night. Heavy drops on the leaves, mercury on swords of iris. Slow waking; a bee thuds on the windowpane.

I walk down the road. Lying, lying, I think. But the truth very plainly acted out. Far toward the sea, the sun-struck foreland, sand and pale green grass; behind, the dark, crowded, thundering mountains. A black cow in the meadow, rather like a bull crowned, but a cow. And always here the sense of the opposite, the still still Sunday (it won't start until after last Mass, said the Sergeant), a few people going by the road, one painted caravan as I sat on the wall and watched: blue, with a yellow door, a little stovepipe capped over the roof, a man, a woman, and a little girl, yellow-headed, on the driver's bench. A spotted dog running behind, hardly having to run, the horse knows him so well, and looks around. His piebald face.

In the hall of the Inn, I knew I should be starting, and asked Mrs. Evans how I could call a hack, as Owen had recommended. "O, there's no taxi," she said, "everybody'll be in Killorglin. But wait, there'll be something."

I was finishing my salmon when she came to find me. "We're in luck," she said, delighted. "The doctor and his wife say they'll drive you in. They're going in ten minutes, and they'll meet you in the lounge." I got up, and we walked down the hall. "I'll see to the shutters," she said. "Don't open them, whatever time you come in. I keep them bolted against the Puck people. Come along here then." She showed me how to let myself in, along the side of the house; she put the key, heavy and ornate, into my hand. It was warm, the metal. I saw myself in the pier glass, tall, big, black-haired, my gray dress with the rose-purple threads in it and the silver metal threads. I knotted my huge square yellow scarf at my throat. I wasn't carrying my camera, but I put my notebook in my pocket, and took the American sunglasses—deep green at the top, pale at the bottom of the panes, from Howard Johnson's. I put them in my bag.

They were in the lounge, three of them. "And Mr. Chris Dermot!" said Katy, remembering in time. "Mrs. Hilliard; Dr. Hilliard." Tall, standing loosely, he smiled at me; in his amazing coloring, the red hair almost rose-color, almost gold-red, the lost color of the Elizabethans, his legendary hair. He smiled his thin and penetrating smile, almost to the bone. His wife was sitting in a square chair, chestnut-brown in her skirt and her hair, with dark red glints made redder in that room of green and leaf-patterns. Long hand offered; pale eyes, ringed around the pale iris, pale but announcing darkness. Both man and wife very slender, flickering, curious, still. Their friend was more usual in his look. Dark green jacket, dark hair and eyebrows run together in one line across; short, wary, held in, but moving forward now, asking why I was going to Puck Fair, I, an American. We're fools to drive a car anywhere near there, aren't we? he said, but here we go.

We got into the green Morris, the doctor and I in the front seat, and stopped at the petrol pump across from the Inn. The man at the pump gave us that greeting of the roads, the easy sideways toss of the head. Dr. Hilliard stood by his car, quiet, while the four gallons poured in. I liked the way he was standing, finely articulated in his bony resting stance. I liked his eyes, in the light clear, brook water two feet under; his clear-skinned face and hands: the leather patches on his jacket elbows.

He got in and swung the car around on the empty road, past

Dooks, the railroad crossing, the golf course, and the Caragh bridge with its six arches. A knot of men at the crossroads.

"All men," said Dr. Hilliard.

"Going to the Fair," said Chris.

"Going to the dances."

"They are."

"You know what they'll do there?" the doctor said.

"What will they?" his wife said, with an inflection that made me turn and smile. Dr. Hilliard looked at me, and back at the road.

"Ireland is the most repressed country," he said. "Highest incidence of alcoholism, lowest of syphilis. At dances, the men gather round and swill; the women sit on the other side, undanced with."

"Dr. Hilliard..." I began.

"She *will* call me Doctor," he said. "Katy's a darling, but I'm Mr. Hilliard, Nicholas Hilliard. I'm a psychoanalyst," he said, looking at me to see how I was taking it. "An English analyst practicing in Dublin."

"There's a mythological beast for you," said his wife.

"Liadain's Irish, of course," he went on. "That's the marriage that'll save us."

"As am I," said his friend. "In the civil service, and I don't know who'll be saved by it."

Nicholas Hilliard was a journalist before he was an analyst, a reader at M-G-M for a while; he lives in Dublin, Liadain and he and their five children, four girls and the youngest a boy. I smile. Liadain says that he'd better tell me that he worships the head of the Irish Psychoanalytical Society, and she chants: Jon-a-than Han-a-ghan. Jaunty.

He's making a religious bridge for Freud, says Chris. Freud's not accepted. Jung's beginning to be accepted—the Dominicans use his work—but, Chris adds, Jung "ratted." Look at the correspondence, he says; you can make psychoanalysis popular if you leave out childhood sexuality. Well, maybe not in Ireland. Ireland's a backwater. You know what has done most to introduce analytical ideas? The films. But that scene's typical, he says, jerking his thin, strongly corded neck at the past road. Groups of boys at the crossroads, jeering at lovers who walk by. The priests with their torches walking the roads at night.

O, and he said, Americans who come here. Two Americans came to be analyzed. Two homosexuals, they were. All right, I said, but come here prepared to live, a year or two anyway. I never thought they'd be back, but they came back, by ship, both of them, and all their pots and pans as well. No, I said, that's not the idea, you're not to live together while you're being analyzed, the first thing we've got to find out is how each of you really wants to live. They were furious, you know what they said? "If you were any good, you'd be riding in a Cadillac." He threw back his head, laughing. In a moment he said, But really, here. Here, in the Kerry women, you see lack of love. Frigid women.

Children got on them by drunken men, said Liadain.

They're used for heavy work, Chris put in.

Sex is disconnected. It's all loathing.

In Ireland, said Nicholas, we have everywhere the problem of hatred. Everywhere. All energy is seen in that.

And everything a sin, said Liadain. If you look in the mirror, I was told, it's a sword in Mary's heart.

17

WE CAME across the bog-land to the Killorglin station. Under a low sky of dove-gray, promising rain. The road at the beginning of town was crowded with cars and donkeys. They've come in by horse-rail, said Liadain, and donkey-rail, seeing the frail carts. Six children, barefoot, across the road, lined up at a long green fence to watch the donkeys. A lorry broken down, with its hood open, in front of Duffy O'Shea's garage, the headquarters of the Puck Fair Committee. The Oisin ballroom, signs and bunting up, prepared for the dance tonight.

"Where would you like us to take you?" Nicholas asked. "We can drop you anywhere."

"Aren't you going to the Fair?" I asked. I could hear a stammer come into my voice.

"No," said Nicholas Hilliard.

"What are you going to do?" I asked.

He put his hand on the blue morocco book, stamped in gold, that was exposed before me in the doorless glove-compartment. "Read Browning," he said.

"Browning wouldn't."

He looked at me, his eyes glinting. Then he swung the wheel over and parked the car, along the fence. A gray donkey kicked the green-painted palings, and the fence rang with the kick.

18

RINGING from the sound—the hoof clapped against the long fence of palings—we got out of the car. Long ago, the fence had been painted green; but beaten, weathered, stained, its rings, writings, pictures stretched to the corner. Mountains and faces emerged in the stains, lines indicated the tilted streets of cities seen from the air, and leaps of hazard and crazy profiles with the hills earned through experience on these cheeks, under these eyes. We made our way along the fence, the four of us, for the street itself was nothing like yesterday afternoon's street, easygoing, with a lounger or two at the corner and a man going into a pub. We were heading into a street of many people, urgent for all their laughing and turning. Around the corner and into a street of pubs: O'Connor's, Doyle's, Pat Joy's, The Canberra, Duffy Moroney's. The whole short street full of backs, everybody slowed down now, shoulders hardly moving, a fleet whistle of song going over our heads.

A woman with black eyes, her russet-orange hair falling at a pitch down along her cheeks, stopped me now. Behind her, her two children waited; they watched me. "Hear your fortune, dear?" the woman said to me. Two men in dark jackets pushed past her. She gave way a step, and came back to me. "You have a lucky face, love."

I wanted the fortune, and that surprised me, with a slight stir. Nicholas turned to look into my eyes with a cool glimmer of mock. "Later," I said.

"You'll never find me later," she said, and held my arm. "I like your face, love. I'd like to tell your fortune."

"I'll find you," I told her. I gave her the coin with the bull on it, and asked her name. Mrs. Shaughnessy, she said, and asked was I going to the river.

I looked at the Hilliards. To the river, she repeated. Where the traveling people are. The caravans. O yes, I told her. I'll find you there, she said.

As we passed the door of Pat Joy's, Chris hunched his shoulders, put his eyebrows up helplessly and said, Wait a minute. He ducked into the pub and was out again. As I thought, he said, and turned up the collar of his jacket. A few of my old friends from Tralee, he said. He looked at the three of us and smiled weakly, with charm and intent.

We went in. They were three-deep at the bar, the dark, grainy smell of Guinness over them, keen and soft like a knife in a cloud. The drink would be bitter if it were thin, I thought, discovering my thirst for it in the sound of words and glasses. Its fine black thickness reassures the throat; it surely is only a bitter beginning, like the kick of the donkey at the fence. It sealed in me the days and nights of preparation and the flight and the last nights before, the long sleep after them, the mixed dread and excitement, the waking today and the prologue, the taste and ringing with which things begin.

We'll leave you then a while, Chris.

To meet later, said Chris, come to life.

How will you find us?

There's time till Coronation. I'll find you. At the feet of the King.

Come to Cahill's a minute, I said. Before the river.

Another pub? Nicholas asked. His nostrils went white.

All right, I said. The barracks instead.

We turned the corner in the press; it was still easy enough to walk. Past the heads, over the caps, the blue tower stood up in the Square, tall and flimsy in a wet breeze from the sea, slapping the flags out straight. They slacked again. The striped booths were up; barkers were crying. One on a high keen note, "Airy Mary is back from Tipperary! Airy Mary is back from Tipperary!" Under his voice, the clacking sound, first very fast, then relenting, lowering, running down, the sound of the wheel of fortune.

"You got here," said the Sergeant, coming in, and his scrubbed face brightened at me. The rays of lines were clear and dark in the shadowy room. I introduced the Hilliards. Guards Tobin and Looby nodded. We are looking forward to the procession, I told him, and glanced at my watch.

"O there's time," said the Sergeant. "Puck won't start until after last Mass." He sat down behind the table, and tipped his chair back.

"We'd like to go down to the river."

"Just watch yourself among those tinkers," he said. "And I'd be back in an hour."

"Bring a glass," he said to his man; and broke the label, and poured me a ritual drink.

19

THE IRISH touched my lips, cool, and then branched out in purity of fire, lips, breath, breasts, and reaching out and down, in a concentration more like cognac, in the most noble white strength. The clearest fire of color I have ever seen was when a photographer set up a bank of lights to make a close-up of my left eye, and the blaze went off beside my head. There was the moment of black; and then two flames in sequence, the most intense lime-green, the most appalling lavender, that I have ever seen, burning, beyond all color. Earthly color is the shadow of what I saw.

All other whisky is the shadow of Power's.

It was a short drink; the bottle was open, and stayed so.

We went out. Straight ahead of us, down the hill of the street, the bridge and river were out of sight. Over across was a green meadow, sheep-starred. As we went slowly down, dodging and passing, we could hear the murmur of the crowd separate, and the men at the booths and panel games crying out: "Airy Mary is back from Tipperary!" "Don't excite the ladies, don't excite the ladies!"

20

THE TWO tinker children in the Square. Crying, hot. Each of them clutching with one hand a leg of their father's trousers. Hopeless, unheard sobs. Both barefoot, the boy and the girl; they pull their feet back when the thick shoes come close. Little creatures, the small chubby boy, hair matted like his father's. The thinner girl-child a bit older. One hand rubbing the hot wet eyes. "Poor cheeks," Liadain says. The children do not look at us, they do not look at their father. Cheeks red, streaked with crying, streaked dirty and clean. The father slaps the head of the boy. He makes no sound as he cries. The girl is sobbing still.

Before them the booths: Virgins in plastic, red balloons, the Virgin of Lourdes, roulette, ringtoss, on a rope a football that will break a balloon if you kick it right, a shooting gallery with a target printed on a card, around which people curve in flatter and flatter arcs as the crowd enlarges. Many knots of crouching people playing cards, and great fringes of those standing and watching the cards as the players throw them down. A man with rats and ferrets running over his chest and back, and a contortionist tied in a knot of himself.

The children watch. Tinkers' children, their tawny savage-faced fathers standing still. A few children in their Sunday clothes, girls who wear ribbons in their pulled-back hair, girls who eat cotton candy from the striped red-and-white booth, a boy with a toy trumpet.

The tinkers' handsome bodies. Their fine deep heads; this one's heavy hair curling low over the scarf, his jacket shaped in a thousand rains.

Downhill, past the Bank corner, the *Telefon* sign, the Kodak place, and all the pubs, squeezing down and out of the crush to the bridge over the river.

Gray over the gray Laune, the stone bridge. Five telephone poles pacing the bridge, and the garland of bulbs strung curving between them. The small waves glinted. A fisherman stood, his back to the town, his cast finished, waiting, ready to be alerted, waiting. On the far side, nine white ducks and one speckled duck came to their decision; among the grasses came walking down, and launched themselves, all but two who, remembering hesitation and its values, hung back, until it was clear that they did not care. And sailed themselves too out upon the river.

The carts coming in still and parking on the far side of the bridge. Ass-rail, horse-rail; the farm people arriving.

"Plenty of women, there; six men, two women; eight men, two women; a man and a woman."

"There's dancing, then," Liadain said.

"We'll have a look at the dance halls," said Nicholas, smiling. He had come into the river-stillness, out of everything gathered in this town, into lightness. He smiled in joy, looking past the bridge.

A wide curve of colors edged the riverbank on the far side. A line of painted caravans, around the first bend of the Laune, straightening out and then lost in trees and the sweep of the river.

From the side, they looked round, like rigid wooden covered wagons, but colored, edged and adorned, announcing something wild and daily. The fronts were alike in design, a half-door painted and carved, and over that the open decorated shutters of the upper door. The shafts leaned down to the ground before each door. Each caravan was painted in its own colors, its own design: wild pink and red, dark blue and serene, canary and gold and deep shiny green. They all were the same size.

We crossed the river to the tinkers' side. Looking back, we saw the town rising from its riverbank: Foley's store guarding the bridge, and the street almost solid black with the crowd, the low buildings and now visible, a great tree-shape midway among the houses. What is that, spreading upward, larger than a tree?

On this side, one house, one bird—a gull hanging in air, wings poised open—a garage with its pole and sign before the pump, and the line of the caravans.

And far off to our left, the mountains, that from the town we could not see. Struck with sun, past the clear dove-gray of the soft moist air.

The women squatted variously, talking and smoking by smoldering pies, on caravan-steps; they walked with a graceful noble walk to spread their wash over the bushes. They stood talking on the unclean roadside.

In the mud, in the deep mire, in puddles of black, the children sat and laughed, ran playing. One bent her knees and toileted herself here in the puddle, and ran away, calling. One walked unevenly down the riverbank and went to talk to three horses spanceled there, unable to go far for the hobbles around their hind legs at the fetlocks. Curious horses they were, among this calling of colors of the clothes, caravans, the blond and red hair. The horses all were piebald, the black-and-white mottles running oddly, at variance with their structure and with their long English faces, as if this design of dapples and spots were in protest to their basic system—a logic of running counter, another announcing.

Very few men here. Most of them already in the town, at the booths? in the pubs?

The children ran up. "Coppah? Coppah?" they said, and spoke to each other in some accented speech I had never heard before. We gave them coins—I had some sixpences, the fine hounds on them, and the hares of the threepenny coins. I could see Nicholas and Liadain speak a word to each other. Very secretly, he then spoke to me, advising: change your money, he said, give the children only coppers, you don't mind if I say this, he said, I begin to know you—don't be ashamed to change money in front of us....

A voice was calling behind me, "You came, love, and you said you'd come! Now your fortune!" It was Mrs. Shaughnessy.

Standing with her behind a caravan, near its cooking pie and stewpot at the stone wall, its glass window and louvers over my head, I looked at my palm. But she was looking into my face, her lined, deeply experienced face looking one straight thing at me, sending me a word, repeating and repeating something like a word I could not hear while she talked on rapidly, on one note, putting the phrases of the fortune together. But what she was looking at me was like the knocking that called me from my sleep: a willed, regular, attempting signal. She was speaking—

"You have turned your back on many men," she said, "and many offers, and have worked with your head. You are fond of music and you are fond of company; but much company is not suited to you. Will you have more?" she asked. "Then give me another piece of silver in my hand.... Your danger comes from a woman between brown and black. She is jealous. You will not have the ten children you wanted. Do you understand?"

"Yes, I do," I answered.

"But you will rear three, two boys and a girl. You understand what I mean?...I'd like to look in the crystal ball for you, love," said Mrs. Shaughnessy.

"Maybe tomorrow," I said, and thanked her.

"But you'd like a holy figure?" she went on. "Here, love, no, this is a present from me." She put a pink plastic Virgin of Lourdes in my hand, the palest pink. I thanked her.

She looked beyond me. In the road, her back to us, a little girl about three years old was standing. Her feet and legs were bare, and above, her one clothing, a little dress, almost came to the top of her legs, not quite. She turned around, and at once it was evident that she was a boy, strongly built and frowning bravely.

"Tommy!" called Mrs. Shaughnessy. "Come and we'll find your sister!" She said something in another language, nodded to me, and went down the road to the tilt they lived in—a propped-up shed standing on two feet, a kettle shining under a heap of clothes.

Liadain and I watched them go down. Nicholas was listening to his fortune. "That child could well wear a bigger smock by now," said Liadain. "He's the size of my Una." Of course she has children, I thought. Five. As she spoke, I was asking, "What language is that? Is that Romany?" And Liadain answered, "No. These are not gypsies, they are tinkers—all Irish, the old Irish families that were stripped of their lands in the ancient wars and driven out on the roads—those not slaughtered—and rather than live under rule, they have lived on the roads ever since. Mark their coloring, and their hair, and their Irish faces—they are O'Briens, Sheridans. Great families of the Geraldine wars. They speak Shelta—I don't know any of it, but you'll probably find someone here who does."

Nicholas was walking toward us. He took a smooth-woven cap from his pocket and pulled it on his head, putting his head on one side. He looked like a man who'd had his fortune told.

"What did she tell you?" Liadain asked.

"Can't tell. It would break the charm," he said, grinning.

"Well, I wouldn't break a grand charm for you," said Liadain.

"She said I'd marry soon—"

"Will you now?"

"—That money was waiting for me at home, and that I was

about to go into a business venture which would be a source of satisfaction to my family, particularly the older members," he told us.

"That certainly has the ring!" said Liadain. "Now, if you don't mind, I'll sit on the bridge, at the end here, and find me when you're ready."

The rich carvings on the caravans, the brass corners, and a child sitting on the steps. I asked her name—she was less than two—a blonde, smooth hair, color of rope-end. "Mary Filomena," she said. Her family had come from Dunmanway. We were not taaveys, too, were we? What was "taaveys," I asked. She shook her head; there was no other word. "I'm taavey," she said.

The man leading a black-and-white horse looked at us in ferocious concentration. I know that look: I have it when I am fixed on something else and look at someone, hard, and never see him. He led the horse down the road to the bridge and over, where the deep-green house and the red one made the beginning of the town. Past Liadain on the bridge. We turned back, and she stood as we reached her. The tinker was leading his horse into a side street.

21

A MAN wearing the peaked cap of the railway was sitting beside her. "Vans is it?" he was saying and he jerked his head toward the tinkers' line. "They have hand cars! They throw the ould mattresses and junk in them. And you can be sure that tisn't on the hire-purchase they got 'em. For who'd trust them for that? Money down; and they have plenty too."

He nodded; wise, wise. "Ah, but the real fun won't be till they start fightin'!"

Liadain was innocent for us, and for him. "Would they really have a stand-up fight?"

"Would they what! Would they kill a one! Didn't they kill a

man outside Malla two years back. Took the top clean off his skull, with a bill-hook." He took his cap off; sign of respect. "Two o' them to go for him."

The tinker was across the bridge. We followed as if he were leading us and piebald horse. The three-card tricksters had set up boards, and a black-and-white checkerboard down the street was being overrun. The owners picked up the linoleum on which the checkerboard was printed and fastened it behind the football kick. Sounds of shooting, flat and high, from the gallery-booth. The thump and patter of the football on its rope, hitting the wall and then bouncing rapidly, mathematically. The round football, following its laws. And now the shattered sound as the football finds its mark and bangs the balloon to a small rag of rubber.

The tinker was ahead of us, through the crowd, and gone. Before us the gray Protestant church, disapproving and silent. There was another statement turning round on itself—Are you Catholic? O, most everybody is Catholic in Killorglin.

He had led his horse through a gate in the fairground. The Ferris wheel was climbing, its blue boats full of people and the girls all screaming. All but one who stared white-faced straight before her. On each boat of the wheel, one big work was painted in white. BIRDS ARE BEST. And then again, BIRDS ARE BEST.

"I like what the cars say," I said, mystified.

"It's the name of the fair rides," said Nicholas. "Birds'—the Bird brothers."

"There he is!" The tinker was still holding the rope of his horse. He was waving the other arm in frenzy at a tall and dapper man in a greenish suit, who leaned away from him as he shouted. Then he leaned forward with his hands clasped on his slender cane, drove the point into the earth of the fairgrounds, and, as we came near, he seemed to say a short sardonic phrase to the tinker. He did not answer, but pulled the horse's rope. The horse looked at them with his pale blue eyes, white-blue, a long-suffering color, and allowed himself to be drawn back through the crowd.

The dapper man spat between his teeth. We were quite close

to him now. He had blue flat eyes, at once round and malicious, and terrible stained teeth, a short well-cut nose, and a prodigious long lip. He used his cane to push the back of his hat up. So that it fell forward over his eyes and shaded them. He was with another man in crumpled clothes, and was now saying something to him that I could not understand at all.

"They're not speaking English, are they?" Nicholas asked Liadain. Just then the word "mare" came through very clearly.

"They are," she said, "it's Kerry, and you leave it to me," and asked them something in their own speech. They answered her in pleasure; the speech began to give way for me; I could get whole phrases now.

Liadain turned to us, very hostess. "This is Mr. O'Connor," she said of the man in the green-and-tan Irish mixture. "He is traveling with Mr. Robinson. They've come for the horse fair."

Mr. O'Connor greeted us. "Tinkers!" he said, vehemently. "Or fools who don't know the way to the Post Office.... Well," he said, suddenly mild, "I've got what I've come for; or part of it, anyway," he said, looking harshly, with greed, at Liadain.

"And what have you got?" she asked.

"Twenty old skins," he answered, pointing to the horses, standing very still beside his friend, the Kerryman with the wide eyes and country-style cap.

"And what will you do with them? Let the smallest children ride them in a horse-ring?" asked Liadain, laughing.

"I will not have them in a horse-ring," he said, and he smiled in friendliness at her wit. "I'll be taking them to Belfast tomorrow—or the next day, if it's as good a Puck as it promises—and sell them for dog meat there if the price is good. Or, more likely, ship them to Brussels to the glue-works."

Nicholas and I were standing a little to the side. "I know that Brussels traffic," he said bitterly and quietly.

The man put his hand up to his red tie that leapt out from his stiff white town-collar, and smoothed down the tie.

Nicholas was getting impatient. Liadain glanced at him. He

was moving most carefully; he said a polite word to the other man; over-polite; Liadain stepped back, to begin to leave.

"Puck's for dancing, too, ma'am. Will you be dancing tonight?" He spoke directly to Liadain, and Nicholas shifted as he stood.

"Very likely I shall," she said.

"I will see you tonight so," he said.

"Good-bye now," said Liadain, and turned away. We went back to the gate, into the street that led to the Square, past the window of the living room that was turned into a tea shop. I saw for a moment the black-and-silver stove ("The range that is always in the corner," said Liadain) and the kettle on it, and the pregnant woman beside it under a raw-colored chromo.

"Let's go in," said Liadain. "Let's have tea."

"But we've had tea," Nicholas said.

"O, do let's," said Liadain. "Just for a chance to sit down again," she said under her breath.

We ordered tea and cakes, and the pregnant woman said, "Your first Puck?"

"It is that," said Liadain.

"It's the two-legged Puck, that's what I'm afraid of, for you," her husband said to her. "Gets into your blood, you know."

I looked out the window. All the Fair sounds, the sounds of the booths, but no more.

"You know, that sea-voyage to Brussels—that's the worst of all for the old horses. They keep them alive on the crossing to get a better price."

"He's right," said Liadain.

"We've been trying to get something done about it, in Dublin," he said.

The pregnant woman, at the stove, spoke to us now.

"And have you gone to visit the Puck?" said the pregnant woman. "The kettle is boiling. Wet the tea, Mother," she said to the woman at the door. "Or here, I'll do it."

"That we have not," said Liadain. "Where is he now?"

"Have some bread," she said. "In the contractor's shed, he is, Mr. Houlihan. Help yourself, now."

"That was nice," said Liadain. "I seldom take a second cup."

"You are not fond of tea, so. I don't know on earth what I would do without the cup of tea."

"I am only after my tea," said Liadain, "but I was lost with tiredness from walking. Where is the shed, then?"

"It is at the corner here, and around to the left."

"That's a handsome range you have," said Liadain. It was the classic stove of this part of the country, a great black stove with silver hasps and handles, set in white tile, gleaming around the dense mat black.

"Thank you for that," said the pregnant woman. "May your journey thrive, you and your husband, and your American friend. The salt sea is between Ireland and America. Many have gone; loneliness is often on me, my brothers and my sister have gone to that country."

But today is here, we said, and we left her, and slowly to the corner, and around, down the little trampled alley of earth to the shed.

In the gray afternoon, brown shadow was thrown where the goat was standing. The contractor's wife led us to the entrance of the little shed. A woman was standing at the doorposts, looking in at the gloom.

22

HE STOOD there, waiting. He was much larger and simpler than I had thought he would be, yellow-white in the shadow, with long brushed hair, a thick brushed coat down over his knees, and a bright white poll, curled and brushed, over his forehead between the long back-curved horns. He kept his head down, flattening the nose and the long convex smiling lip, presenting his horns.

They rose thick from his forehead, branching out to left and right, soaring out and beginning to twist in a hint of wide spirals. Corrugated and pointed, without warp, without distortion, no mark on them but the scrape along the left blade, a chart of old war. The seams were along the edges, and the texture of horn seemed at first like that of wood until you saw the laminations by which they were forged, built up, the pattern welded, and the fibrous structure of these swords, harder than any one material, welded of materials of different quality, drawn out, shallow and turned and running the length of the horn; and on the left groove, like a graph recorded by some even sharper sword, or acid, or steely rocks, the scar.

The faces of the horns were stiff-cut, they ran to their jagged edges; smooth as they looked at first, when this unadorned, dominant, luxuriant and waiting king stood in the shadow, they soon showed knots and nodes of formation, and something like strips, something like rings of iron.

He put his head down; now they seemed not welded to his head, but rooted deep in his skull, in his brain, in his eyes which I had not yet seen.

And all the time his tail, lifted and short, was vibrating, shivering in his waiting mood, answering the weapon with his other qualities, nerves, consciousness.

"The smell is killing me," said Mrs. Houlihan's friend. "Won't I be glad when they take him away! What time is it, then?"

23

A WORD went over the crowd, a sound like a strange note in music that quieted them, and opened the roaring of the air to another note, higher, intense, reaching the center of the body and seeming to travel outward to the ears. It was the bagpipes. The spanned music—the high piercing cry and the underdrone, stabbing and wringing, reached us as we stood at the Nolans' window. We looked out at the people through whom we had made our way to the barracks' door. And then upstairs to the rooms, and all the children—Stephanie, the eldest, with Nicholas beside me, and the baby held on Liadain's lap, starting and calling to the piper's music. The Square was filled; packed tight against each other, with the children invisible in the crush, it was impossible for them to move or turn; but they did move, slowly and with enormous difficulty opening a way. At the sides, there were the calls of women pushed against the plate-glass windows. The pipers outcried all. Led by a small boy, saffron-kilted, and wearing a green tartan, his face white and concentrated in tense pride, they thrust their knees out, ringing, snarling, driving their music through the air.

Behind them, rising up from the river, the amazing procession came. Following the pipers, an open truck pushed inch by inch up the hill. Standing just behind the red cab, four young boys in white and green held their spears up and forward toward us; and at the back of the truck, on a bridge of planks, stood the platform—the throne—of the white goat. Four more boys, guardians, spear-bearers, rode the planks; two more stood on the floor of the truck, holding their spears fierce and straight. Two more stood in the corners, at the back. Long strings of pennants rose up from the headlights to poles in the truck, and stretched backward, saffron, white, green and red.

The boys' trousers are green, and their ties; their skirts are white; so are the spears white and green, with silver spearheads made at home. They are all boys of the same size, a size meaning a stage just before puberty or else a small man, ancient and small, a size not seen in northern countries since neolithic times.

The goat is vastly changed. An hour ago, in the shed, he was uncertain, vibrating. Now his time has begun, although he has not yet achieved his place. He stands on his roofed platform, wearing his robe, a green blanket bound and corded with red. Still and firm, he stands, long white waterfalls of fur cover him to his ankles. As he approaches dominion, his white head is held up; the white mane curls forward over his forehead; a cord of great round bells stretches in a curve from horn to horn.

The second truck seems empty for a moment. Then it moves from under the green pennants. A little girl, dressed as a queen, sits there; she makes a center of silence. Receptive, lovely, she is the Green Queen, in green robe and mantle over her shoulders, and her brown hair down her back in little waves and sepia mist. She wears a broad gold crown with big jewels—almost as large as the goat's bells—spaced around, and in front a harp over her round brow. Around the child's waist is the wide girdle of a queen, with gold tab pendant to back and right, coming to points that point down her loins. She is attended by a lady-in-waiting, in green too. This is a young woman.

The goat has begun to take on his new life. A curious shudder goes through the crowd, in recognition. Now they are not watching, they are part of this requirement in the air, where the presence of the Puck, the receptive presence of his Queen, demand acknowledgment.

The music is right before the tower, breaking over all in shrill ripples, an underdrone like a repeated wave, a sort of shuddering. The pipers turn off the Square, and the third truck can be seen.

Bright red, a loud clap of red, the stiff and hieratic bird spreads out his wings. Eagle-beaked, horn-headed, his white eye flame-shaped, he holds out the separate feathers. At his feet rise flames, the same red as he; bright blood, bright fire, and the fire raging up like thorns which could never reach him. I feel myself start, hard against Hilliard's arm, and the points of my breasts stand up: I can see the big word below the red creature. It says PHOENIX, below the painted bird. It is all there: king, queen, and resurrection.

The bird truck swerves, following the goat, the Green Queen, and the pipers. There is a smaller phoenix painted on its door. Then I can see what it is. Grinning, the men in the truck, young and triumphant, stand over brown barrels banded with silver. They grin; they wave their hands; they beg the crowd to wait, while the shallow amber pools on top of the barrels slop over. The truck turns the corner, brimming with ale.

I laugh at myself; Nicholas is saying, "I never heard of Phoenix Ale."

The phoenix is still there, red and eternal.

24

THE PROCESSION forces open the crowd and heads for the Oisin Ballroom. In the Square, the feeling has changed. Short waves of movement disturb the surface, as the impatience builds. A few hand-lettered I.R.A. signs bob up, sink, rise again.

Suddenly—if anything in that slow, tight body could be sudden—a surge develops at the Bank corner, and a Morris appears among the arms and shoulders. Incredibly, it turns into the Square and heads toward the tower. Its wheels cannot turn without crushing the feet of twenty people. Around it, a kind of crunching of space takes place; there must be, between layers of clothing, air layers that can still be compressed. And between flesh, flesh. And joints and sockets. The Morris does advance. The procession is making its way around the town. As the pipes are finally heard again, a double sound, part laugh, part groan, comes from those pressed around the car. Someone has opened its hood, five men throw themselves on it bodily until it becomes invisible and a woman sits her baby on the corner over the taillight.

Sergeant Nolan and Looby are firmly making their way through impossibility to the car. They prevail upon the people who now cover it entirely to lean away from its tail and toward its headlights, create a continuous opening through which it is pushed back to the Bank corner, and around it, as the procession reaches the blue tower.

The step dancing, the accordion display from the States, even the renewal of the sale of tickets for the Miniature Sweeps, cannot quiet the crowd in the Square. The loudspeakers are turned up farther, and the photographers push forward on the platform. Mr. Houlihan leans out from the platform to the truck with the white goat. "All right, boys!" he says, and the goat, shed and all, is slid over the planks on which it rested and onto the lower stage of the tower.

From the microphone, the first lines of a song are magnified frightfully:

Your eyes
Are the eyes
Of a woman in love—

and then cut off.

The speaker begins. "This, according to ancient tradition, is the finest, most majestic he-goat to be found on the slopes of the MacGillycuddy's Reeks. Some say that this is a Cromwellian goat, who saved the town of Cill Lorgan when it was a hamlet of thatched huts. But we know that Cromwell and his generals never set foot in County Kerry.

"Some say the origins of this festival belong in the mists of antiquity, that the area around Killorglin was the scene of many of the legendary exploits of Diarmiud and Graine, and that it was in their time that the first goat ruled from his tower. We need scarcely say that there is nothing on record to support the belief of a pre-Christian origin.

"No; more likely that the story as we have it is the real one, the story of Dan O'Connell and the local landlord Blennerhasset, here in 1808, Mr. Harman Blennerhasset, and how the Liberator helped Blennerhasset to levy the tolls, even though the Viceroy of Dublin had made the tolls unlawful."

One cheer, like hysteria, from the pink doorway of Stephens Champ. The photographers are climbing up. The I.R.A. signs have vanished.

The speaker continues: he wishes to thank those responsible ... he begins lovingly to read the names of the Committee. The sky has turned bruise-purple over the gray, where the crowd slopes downhill; far over and across, the field on the other side of the Laune is a fever green, vibrating yellow and red. Black cattle in a constellation.

He is finishing. A man in a blue serge suit begins to climb the tower with something in his hand. It lengthens behind him, the rope to raise the goat. He turns at the second stage and smiles thickly down. The tower sways from side to side of a plane, like a creature on water skis.

The speaker is introducing the Green Queen: "Kathleen Corkery, our ten-year-old Queen, and her lady-in-waiting, the ever-charming Miss Nuala O'Sullivan, Queen of the festival." Up in our window Stephanie says to me, "That's my friend, that's Kathleen."

The lady-in-waiting looks desperate; her face goes crooked in an embarrassed one-sided simper at the photographers. She is thinking only of herself.

But the Green Queen, with a young and powerful gesture, takes the tall crown from the hands of her lady-in-waiting. The crown had never been offered. She is giving it, the Queen has assumed the potency of the gift. She looks at the goat. She gives his head the high crown, buckling it about the base of his horns. The power of her clear voice carries high and young; she says, "I crown you King Puck."

"The only king of Ireland!" sings out the chairman. "Hip, hip—" and the cheer arrives.

25

I LOOKED at the men as they began to pull on the ropes. Almost everybody had cleared away from the lowest floor of the tower; no girl pipers, no twins from the States. There were five men involved in the Elevation of the King. One of them was now standing near the microphone, lifting one foot and then the other in a quickened rhythm, a step dance hastening on as the goat's platform began to rise. The dancer shut his eyes, his dance was fast now and he was lost in it. His back was to the mike and its long cord dwindled away from him in silence. I watched him dance, his knees lifting and lifting as his body stayed almost still and his feet went free, up and down.

Two other men were pulling on the rope that went up past the second floor of the tower to the pulley wheel above the third floor. The first floor was solid, the men were pulling against the wood beneath them and against the rope, whose end still coiled in slack circles at their feet. The second floor had an oblong opening cut in it, just big enough to let the goat and his platform rise up through it as through a doorway. The third and highest floor was not a floor at all; or it was a floor of air, with a double cross of planks running over it. At the meeting-place of this cross the king would stand. The timbers were not new. They were freshly painted and bright blue, but you could see the nail holes of other years. And the three ladders, set against each floor, looked well-used and familiar.

Two more men stood steadying the platform, one on each side as it began to rise. It swayed, about four feet above the flooring. I was looking down at the white King, his green robe over his back and the bells slung between his great horns swaying from side to side. He backed two small steps, as far as he could move, backing in time with the dancer beneath him. He was backed against the railing of his platform. I could see his short tail tremble, and then go firm as the swaying stopped. He was rising, smoothly, in strong pulsations. Circle after circle of rope fell as he rose, like the coils of music as a great bell rings. No sound came from the Square. We watched him rise in the strong silence, as the dancer paced the rising, and the men pulled hard on their rope, drinking the rope down to earth as the King went up.

He was before my eyes now. What is wrong? I thought suddenly, in clumsiness of soul. Is there something the matter with him that they are so large, so heavy? Surely they would not choose a Puck who had something the matter with his sex.

The huge white balls were before my eyes, great in their power and whiteness. The life of the King was in them, making reasons for the eye's glint, the curl of lip, the hard spread of bone lifting out of his forehead. Energy bulged here, a double bulge robed in the smoothness of white fur, hidden and trumpeting, open and recondite, worlds creating worlds, something secret and understood. I laughed at myself in pleasure and triumph. Wrong! He swung there, strong, white, the crowned world rising up through worlds, crowned by a girl's arm, still and held in his kingship, with the great bells ringing slung between his horns, the great testicles slung between his legs.

They lifted their eyes in silence, all of us looking, looking, as some strength poured out upon the air. Everyone looking up at the King on his tower; all but one woman whose face was fastened sideways, staring across all the faces at someone with a camera. I looked up again at him. He was larger than before, braced and powerful. He turned his head from side to side, and around backwards to where we watched from the windows. His eyes glinted yellow. A long strong scent, a great pennant of smell of goat, goat of the world and the world of goat in his kingship, on his height, streamed across all of us, flowing on air. The huge cheer went up: "King! Puck!" Up, on the air, a sound that was a tower around a tower, in the filled and male upper air of the King.

26

THE CHILDREN were taken off down the hall to bed, protesting as they went. Stephanie took the child next younger, and Mrs. Nolan drew one by the arm and carried the baby asleep on her left shoulder; she smiled at me, flushed and busy while I stood doing nothing at the window. They disappeared down the dark hall. Outside, the colored bulbs brightened as the sky went dark: blue, yellow, red, green, yellow again. Something was waiting to burst. Two drops of rain fell on the sill.

Steps sounded like rain behind us, and we turned. Chris was running up the hall. "Still here?" he said, balancing in the doorway. "I tell you who I've found: that's Bryan MacMahon. He's a good writer."

"Yes he is," I said. "I know that story of his, of Paddy who came home...."

"Two men in Ireland can speak the tinker's language as if it was their own," said Chris. "MacMahon's one. You come along and see him."

Paul Rotha had been sure that Bryan MacMahon would turn up. "He won't be able to stay away from Puck Fair," he said to me in London, after the theater.

"Where is he now?" I asked.

"In what back room? O'Sullivan's," said Chris. "Come along."

We said good night to the Nolans in the living room, in the bathroom where the tub was full of clothes waiting for attention, in the bedroom where Stephanie was hearing prayers. "See you tomorrow," I said. "And your Green Queen was fine." She looked up at me with a look of joy.

As we went out the door, the warm damp smell of many wet coats came up the stairs. Halfway down, the crowd began; they were dancing in the doorway. A burst of music; and then the instruments drowned out by the laughing and the talk as we went down, a great voice sounding continually, one voice saying some slowly developing thing. Then another four or five notes of music, and the sound overpowered it again.

"Maybe O'Sullivan will want to show you Puck Martyr," Chris said. "O God, I hope not," he went on. He twirled through an opening we had not seen in the route. Small, nimble, he found the places, opened them for a second and led us through.

A huge woman in white, with pointed breasts and vast hips, had cleared a circle around herself with her dance. She was stamping it out, a florid ingenious welcome to the man she brought to her. She made a pause, the length of the two breaths, and pulled in another man, letting her partner go, and holding to herself the new young man while the music poured down over them from the loudspeaker on the tower. Her old partners curved around her, clapping and waiting their next turn. She threw back her head as the music changed: *Here*, it said, and shook out a flag and insistence of its own stamping, Ravel's stamping, the "Bolero" making its snakes of sound; the red snakes against the black side of the Spanish ship. She was stamping in her large clear fervor, taking another man as her five waited their turn. We passed around the circle, the circus, the curve, taking the edge and going in the doorway of this pub. It took ten minutes to move these few yards, rocking among these dancers, who roared and put up their faces to the beginning of the rain. They roared, wanting night, wanting music and space to dance; and much more than moving and turning, wanting now closeness in which, if anyone moved, the thrill and heat of this closeness under the King carried along an unknown wave.

"In here!" said Chris. He looked at the three of us, his pointed face quick, his look darting to the mirror and along the bar in the mirror. "You have a drink," he shouted, burrowing in among the arms and elbows, "I'll fetch him," and disappeared past the fine thick man, who gave way a half-inch until Chris passed.

We got our drinks before we saw him again. He was only three or four men down the bar, talking to someone hidden from me by a huge man who looked like Gyppo in *The Informer*. Chris's face was deep red; he glanced at me, and started to push his way back. He was shaking his head at all of us, but his look came back to me—he wanted to see how I would take it. Even standing beside us, he had to shout over the voices.

"I'm sorry," he said to all of us, "it wouldn't work, I couldn't— He says," he reported directly to me, "that he doesn't care to meet you: he says 'just another American to say things derogatory to the Irish people.'" He rolled the line, stamping the syllables in their own bolero.

"I'm sorry," I repeated. "I begin to see." I could feel the dark blush go up my bosom and my cheeks. I'm not like that, I thought, and my jaw tingled.

"Come out, then," said Nicholas. He took my arm, and Liadain began to make her way to the door. "We'll go to the dance hall."

"Dancing, darling?" Liadain said to him in the street. She lilted it. She asked it as if it held five questions at least.

There were many pairs dancing in the Square, and more single dancers, too, performing alone, head thrown back, and then pulling anyone in. Women danced rock-and-roll together. A tall, orange-headed man in a thick Irish sweater flung his arms around me in a cloud of the smell of seashore and the rain. He had spun me around facing the tower. The Puck stood there, white as if struck by lightning, white as the Delacroix horse in the painting, the gleams of red and blue raining down from the bulbs, all his flags flapping about him at the corners of the square tower.

"Come along!" Nicholas called, fastening his look on us as we danced. The speakers were turned up, and full blast from them came, "Shake, Rattle and Roll"; the steady beat compelled the dance. Even as you moved in the slowest, most restricted, most pushing and limited of purpose walk up the streets of pubs. Even as you walked around the corner, the jangle of the music tore into the marrow; then an Irish song unknown to me, and around the corner to the Oisin. The music changed to "Big Man," and we went into the dance hall.

Big man yesterday
But boy you ought to see him now.

The crowd gave way, and Chris and Liadain, Nicholas and I walked onto the floor. Liadain and Chris began to dance, Liadain a little taller than he, but swaying, graceful, losing height and allowing his compactness to take on strength. Nicholas said, at my ear, "We'll have a dance, and then we'll all go home—go back to the Inn."

"O no," I said. "I'm staying."

"Surely not," he said, and the crowd for a moment pushed him back and away from me.

As I felt myself say "I'm staying," a movement of nervous certainty swung me away from that moment and everything that had gone before, whatever I had been feeling, known and unknown, and into another state, the deeper water of what I had come for. I swung into a movement that had begun when the King was crowned, when the Green Queen lifted out her young girl's arm with the gold power, and gave it to him, and turned in almost the same gesture, looking over her shoulder in ecstasy to where I stood beside the girl who was her close friend. No, before that, when the procession moved slowly through the crowd in the Square and king, queen, phoenix could first be seen. No, before that, when we stopped at Killorglin and the lines and stains and creases in the green fence suddenly reminded me of all the people, all the threads, in my life. No, long times ago, in all the movements of the rousing of these storms of passion, rages and lightnings of wish, storms of action, all narrowed down to my life in these last few hours with these new three friends.

I looked at the dance room. The Oisin was a movie house the rest of the year. All the chairs had been taken into the back halls and stored folded away for Puck, and the floor throbbed to the live music of

MARTIN FITZGERALD AND HIS ORCHESTRA
(LIMERICK)
with the Dynamic Vocalist, "Shane,"
just returned from the U.S.A.
after a TV and broadcasting tour.

Chris was standing before me. We danced, with a curious distance and wrongness between us, as if the slight distance of my height above him had been thrown into endless dimensions. He was just too distant for me, just too short. He was saying, "You might be Rumanian, with those pointed eyebrows and the cleft in your chin. Are you?"

What an ass, I thought. "—born in New York," I heard myself say, from some great distance. He was going on. "Your eyes change color—I suppose you know. Often, they do. Gray, and then blue. Now green," he said. "Do you know when they're changing?"

He was leading me badly; or I was not following. It was as if he was moving only from the knees down. Let the music do it all for both of us; but the music would not, in its stilted imitation of jazz. Chris would not. I felt strange, estranged from all of them, on a wave of the opposite just after a wave of strength. I felt awkward, in the center of Chris's awkwardness with me. Why should I let him set clumsiness as the style of our dialogue? "Only when I am told," I answered him, too late.

I'm staying, I thought, and felt absolutely alone. Bereft.

Nicholas and Liadain were dancing, perfectly, quite slowly, doing a step of a generation ago, taking more room than anyone else. Close. They danced over to where we stood as the music ended. I went to Nicholas, as the others moved away again. Now it all changed, fluid and clear, Nicholas and myself and the dance knew one creature, were one creature, declaring something the music was, something the tower outside was. The goat on the black air. I saw Liadain far across the floor.

"Surely you'll come back to Glenbeigh?" said Nicholas.

I shook my head, and began to say good night, good night. We stood at the green fence, pushed by many people, among the donkeys and the cars. The faded green boards were lit from across the way, softened, full of forgetting of their stains and multitudes. We would meet in the morning and come into town together. We would leave word at the desk with the toy currach and the Waterford glass. Good night, Liadain; good night, Chris. Nicholas, good night.

The side street went on, full of dancing. I edged back toward the Square. It was different, not being four-square with two men and another woman.

"Put your nose around the door, John—"a voice said, through the roar.

And another—"And now four large coins in your hand, held tight."

The big man in the Irish sweater was like a wall before me. His mouth was on my mouth. The smell of the sea, the taste of deep sea. Gulf Stream of whisky. I turned from him, and went down the street.

A tinker woman, the young tinker woman who had stopped me long before. I wanted to ask her something, and put my hand on her finely muscled forearm. "Tell me," I said, "the goat—why do your people say he is up there, on the tower?"

She looked into me. "The goat is the king over all."

27

SMELL OF goat in the Square, smell of ale. Crubeens, periwinkles eaten with ale. The American Cheer Girls, back on the platform in the rain, huddled and talking something over. But all over the Square, covered striped booths, barrows of small and salable plastics trundled away. The drunken lout who had tried to lie on the Morris as it was pushed inch by inch into the people packed tight—now he is pushed, propped, supported and hauled along by three women with their skirts pulled half around, as if by an unanswerable torque. A most answerable torque.

Under the goat's tower, in the colored light of the string of bulbs, a man turns, gross and alone, his arms stiff out, his many shadows holding their arms out in a spiny wheel around him. As he turns to me, I see his huge face, his tongue lolling out, sick, too thick to be held in his mouth, and around his neck the sign that reads: DISABLED FROM BIRTH. Beyond the Square, out of bounds of all the pub rooms, a light burns in a street shop that has sandwiches and tea. A small boy is in there. I go in and sit at a middle table. In the gloom, the boy is pouring tea for a sodden drunk, insane and smelling of Guinness. The boy is small and his teapot is immense. The drunk reaches and falls on his elbow on the table, his head lurching. Polite, quiet, in fear and knowledge, the small boy goes on pouring tea, canting the teapot at a friendly angle, with his whole body pulling away from the table and the man. In the silence, a struggle goes on, a struggle so intense that the boy's arm looks lengthened in it, as he pours his arm appears longer and longer. He gets the cup full. The drunk inhales his tea at one pull, and his head falls, knocking the table. I hear the knock; the boy and I look at each other. He smiles, a blue-eyed total smile, and pours my tea and hands me my sandwich now. The drunk gulps, gulps again, and snores; the boy walks, having been paid, in as wide an arc as he can manage, crowding the wall and disappearing around it into the dark room beyond. A door shuts.

28

A HIGH sexual laugh. Whinnying, nickering, the winds of night. Laughter of seven people. A dragging sound upstairs; who is being pulled across the floor? A bottle lands and splatters into glass knives.

Keen yelling, a palpitation of the throat of a beast exactly the same size as Killorglin.

Cries, sounds of women. Panting, lapping, racing noises. The goat leans down in the bright light, he begins to eat his cabbages.

29

AT CAHILL'S I go behind the bar and set to washing glasses. Peter says, "We thought you'd never," and Noreen, watching me, after a few minutes says, "You might like it upstairs."

Every room has been turned into a pub. The furniture has been pushed upstairs, to the third floor, as far as it will go. "We'll make some money, yes, and I expect to lose twelve pounds—of weight, that is—these three days," Peter adds. It's going well, he says. The yearling colts are going for about £26; the two-year-olds bring about £45. "Give over, let her go upstairs, Peter now," Noreen comes by saying, and rubbing the bar with her rag, while the boys bring out seventeen Guinness, and eleven Irish, and twenty-three more Guinness.

Upstairs, a girl is pouring Jameson. "The Stork Americans," she says, winking at me. I go behind the bar quickly, duck my head, and wash glasses.

"Are you a native?" the tallest man in the room says, pinching the girl's behind. "I am that," she tells me. He is clearly American; his English jacket, the sunglasses in his pocket, tinted deeper green at the top, his narrow tie.

"I'm not a native," said a long-legged girl in a vanilla lace dress. Where have I seen her? Or is it her picture, eyes almost closed, on a magazine cover?

"She's not, either," said the fat man, bald and gleaming—head, eyes, teeth, all highlights. Pointing at me. While I drink my

Power's, polish the glasses, all gleaming beneath my hand. And glints of talk. We were sitting around the Stork, they were saying. Pickets outside?—I don't know... and Sherm said somebody was going to the Horse Show. Sounded like an idea.... I got on the phone.

"They had their own train," said Peter, washing glasses beside me. "Seventy miles an hour across to Killarney, slower during mealtime."

The talk went on, in broken, glassy splinters. We slept on the plane, someone was saying. The fumes of the Irish curled around the room, golden and fiery. "I saw you while the poor old goat went up," said the big man to me. "You and your yellow scarf in the window."

"Did you see the Horse Show?" I asked him.

"Did we ever! By the grace of Seconal on the plane, and those spansules—what are they, Dexedrine, Dexamyl?—all through the evening. That Horse Show is way out—Elsa was there, and Huston, he's shooting *John Paul Jones* around here somewhere. He's rebuilt something to be early Portsmouth... a clean shipbuilder's town, he says. Well, he was born there. I saw some of the stills. You'd hardly know it's Ireland. Who was that skinny bird with you?" I told him about Nicholas. The girl in vanilla lace came over to us, long-legged, teetering.

"I like shrinkers," said the bald man. "Here, this is Miss Lorda Taylor, named for the store, isn't that a gasser? She wanted to know about your friend—he's a witch-doctor, baby."

The girl had heard one word of what we were saying. She leaned forward slowly, following her own rhythm, her own music. Slowly. The absolute perfection of skin, of the cut of all the planes of her face and throat, the marvelous collarbone with its central cup of blue shadow, the curve to the breast. Her long eyes were amazed.

"*Ireland?*" she said. "Are we in Ireland?"

The chief Stork had had a talk with Duffy O'Shea. I'd like to glamorize the Fair, sure, he said, but what can you do? Slapstick. A couple of tricks. Amateurs! he said, and the word hurled across like a thrown dart. That's what I hate—amateurs.

A current was coming into the room, and the press of Storks gave way before it—two boys carrying a case of Bushmill's between them. "Put it on the train," said an American. "We'll push on to Killarney. No place to stay here—not on this whole God-forsaken patch. We'll see what's over there. Someone in this crowd's got a hard on to buy up some island in their lake—he don't know it, but I say goose the price a little, it's yours. I thought there might be like something here, a Mardi Gras format, maybe a spectacular in it. But what can you *do*?" He looked around in despair, said something to me, invited me to come along with them. He was startled when I refused, but only for a second. In slow motion, they collected each other; swaying with very steady heads, they made it to the door and down the stairs. Only one slipped, and only for five or six steps. The Bushmill's cleared a passage for them. Their noise was swallowed up in the one buzzing, roaring, spiraling sound that now filled everything.

Glasses gleaming, squeaking clean under my hands.

I was at the door in a great flow of moist night air and mist. Over the rooftops, throwing a clump of daisies on a live patch of roof into silhouette, the moon appeared, peach-color, gibbous. Beside me the tall tinker again, kissing me; we were dancing before the pub, and up the hill to the tower. The speaker and its music were long silent; it was long past music.

We stopped under the string of lights. Three men came out of another bar. They stopped, to see what we would do. "Come with me," said the tinker. "Tom bèar, bura bèar you are. Don't misli with them." The warm secret tongue... it was perfectly clear what he was saying. He threw a glance of contempt, out of fire and secrecy. "The nidias of the ken-gater don't granni what we're a tharyin'."

"What's ken-gater?" I asked.

"Drink-house," he said, grinning. "They don't know what we're saying." Neither do I, I started to answer. But it was not true.

"Get!" he was saying. "Wait! I'm a minker, and I think you have known us? Spoken our taral, our speech? Can you bug Shelta? Have you traveled with minkers?"

"No—" I began, and at that moment I wished I had. From then on, as when I was a small girl I ran off with circus people, with the lion Caesar and his trainer, and the twins in the circus on Long Island; staying only the day, and going home at last, to find that all the families, and the police were searching.

"Let her be!" yelled a drunken muffled voice behind me, and the horse-trader O'Connor pushed through the people around us and flung himself on the big tinker. The tinker took the full impact on his broad neck and shoulders. With one throwing, twisting movement that seemed to involve only the top of his body, he hurled O'Connor around and down, flat on the ground, still spinning sideways with the torque. O'Connor yelled out "Duka yar!" Two men beside me threw themselves into the fight, and the knot began to roll downhill, thrashing; the sound of blows landing made a drumming. The crowd pushed backward and away from them, clearing a way.

From the bridge, tinkers ran uphill, joining in. Couples would fight and be separated easily, a kind of good humor seeming to prevail among the heaviest slugging. Women joined in; I saw real fighting begin among four women, who, again, were easily separated. Six more began, and one threw a bundle she was carrying to a friend who was walking behind her, asking to tell fortunes.

"That's beautiful slinging of the baby!" said an old man at my side.

From the crowd, a dark tall man appeared. He was young, with piercing and distant eyes, and with a new white bandage around his hand. His right hand. He leapt toward O'Connor, rose off the ground in the sailing arc of a great dancer, and reached O'Connor's cheek at the end of his leap. I saw him land on his feet as the tinkers closed in, shouting, "Gifan glader!"

"Something about horses," said the voice over my head. "Chiseler, too," as the fight went down toward the bridge. A woman was swept into a doorway and half-pushed, half-carried up the stairs by four men. "Well," said the voice, "our night is almost done."

The sounds were all around us, filling the town, in all the black streets, and under the colored bulbs. Far out into the fields, the screams of this release, the turning loose, harshness drawn of breath and the gasping, singing, sweating drunken cry.

The man beside me was tall; I had seen him in the crowd, his deep stare when the King was crowned. He had a bottle in his hand, and gave it to me: the gold-belted Power's bottle. I tilted my head and drank, my head back. The goat was above me still, looking into my head, his whisky eyes looking through the world.

"You're not from here?" said the tall man. "You're not staying here?"

"No, at Glenbeigh," I said, and gave him his bottle. He drank long. He took the bottle in one arm and me in the other, and we danced the length of the Square.

"And I'll drive you home when you're ready," he said.

A mist was falling over the Square, and a hint of morning in the blackness.

"Almost, now," I said.

"Come then," he said. "The car's in Duffy O'Shea's garage."

30

WE PASSED the doorway and saw them there, together and laughing, together that did not reach us except as a long pennant of goat reek and hoarseness, together in a long and crowing cry.

"That's as they say," said the tall man.

A firkin and a fuck
And that makes Puck.

And into the fields we drove, with the cry of couples, the cry of the roosters before dawn, the stillness of the mist.

He was tall, adept, sure—Kevin Foley, who keeps the railroad crossing at Mountain Stage.

On the way, the mist deepened—sea fog, like the nights sweeping through Golden Gate; heavier, Connecticut ground fog in summer and as white; beard of Puck, old white-beard that rules the night and the *prodromos* of morning, with its cry.

You could come to America, I told him.

"And what would I be in America? A sweeps?"—He looked at me suddenly with the hopelessness of the cut-off men, the men in doorways, the men who come from their railway crossings and want something in their fantasy.

"You speak of the writings," he said. "My dad told me of one who stayed at Mountain Stage, at Philly Harris', long ago. Eyes of gentleness, a down-drooping moustache. He made plays and listened to stories. He went to Puck Fair one year, though he came later in the summer, the other Kerry times. Synge, his name was."

He craned forward to drive in fog. The headlights were failing, and he hugged the center line. Then he let out a cry.

"Arragh, it's Dooks."

Dooks is the town before Glenbeigh.

31

INTENSE sudden fear in the fog. Color of the fog beginning to change, but it cannot be getting lighter; it is only some change of emphasis, dread turning to dread, the road and garden and house surrounded. Foley and I shaking in the shaking garden. His headlights failed, he dares not turn the engine off; and is gone up the road. The garden drags at my legs, I am at the side door, my key scratches in the lock. It will not turn, it is made of flakes of metal, it will dissolve before it turns in this insubstantial lock. I am in the room.

The silent, scented room. In the grate, threaded gold, the turf burning, silent where the chocolate fiber burns upward without a word. Coal, wood utter in the flame the sounds of the forest. This peat burns speechless in the silence of the bog, ferny in fire, little streams of flame in the brown earth of this soft bed, this fuel, contemplation.

On the little table she has put out for me coffee in a thermos and little darling watercress sandwiches.

The room is dark. Remember how she said, "I bolt my shutters against the Puck people"—?

The loneliness strikes me. I think of Jonah, Ella going to Peking this week, my young son far away. The clump of turf settles, it is the core of this night, fertile of fear.

A great stir at the window, beyond any fireplace, any bolt and lock. I lie still on my bed, elbows pulled in against my colding sides. It rustles, shakes the door, through my closed eyes I see the body of a man, a big tinker hero, a young god, fear, goat-face wise and overpowering. Look of desire in his—look of lust and . . . not glare of anger in his eye, but lust and speed, like the "queer eye" of the racing cyclist, of the man at crisis, coming, all desire, all perversion, all grace, made and found and resolved in the other. In himself. Lonely, with a world of desire in my skin, in these walls, within this fog, with Nicholas and Liadain in bed somewhere here, the coupled endless thousands in every lying stance, in every combination, and thousands coupled in my life, in me, the white beard streaming over us, the tense and potent desire streaming over all, flame, flag, power that is nothing, dust, nothing, until it reaches.

With a pulse of color, the last leap of daybreak.

The fear transformed.

And I began to wake. And fell asleep as I woke.

THE DAY OF THE FAIR

1

I SLEPT; a different sleep, diving far past the rout. In the calm and nimble morning, woke. Only two hours further. Many sea-birds making tall crying. I opened the shutters; nobody. The glistening garden, the flashing lights of the sea. I dressed in my gray wool dress, and tied its belt, around my neck tied the bright blue Persian beads, and left my black raincoat on the chair in front of the cabinet that held Mrs. Evans' silver. The dining room was just closing, but they gave me strong tea, three cups of it, and the rough grainy sugar full of small lancing shadows and glitter. Then they brought six strips of Irish bacon, the best I had ever tasted, and the fine thick restoring bread.

The Hilliards and Chris were in the corridor. I could hear Chris laugh in answer to something, and Nicholas put his head round the dining room door. "Just in time," I told him, and put aside the plate. "The tea's still hot."

"O *come* on," he said. "You've been asleep for hours."

"Not so many."

"I thought you were going to stay awake all through Puck."

We drove in over the road that hangs and dips and rises again, festoons on the brown soft sponge of bog. "It was built level, and then—" Chris said, making his hands ripple. The bog-smell, gentle, aromatic, and everywhere.

2

DROVERS on the road as we reached Killorglin in the drizzle of rain, so light it was simply a stir in the air. Drovers in their boots with their slender sticks, heading the cattle to left and right. Any cars or horse-rails driving through today may forget about the rules of the road; they use the center. The sides belong to the black Kerry cattle; short and small, all of them, like the first wooden cows and bulls of childhood as they push and are turned and beaten and compelled by the urgent rods. They turn their shapely heads, pressing, the black cattle, moving into a wedge-shaped herd to let the car go past.

The sky streaked gray-yellow, gray-orange, and wet. Where the road had been jammed black with dancers, now the black animals pushed and crowded, beaten over the rumps and sides, bellowing, a black sound.

"Let's go around," said Liadain. The fence was green over the heads of cattle. No car could stop among these horns.

At the bridge over the Laune we parked the car. The river was gray in the drizzle, gray with slants of metal blue, and one fisherman waited, pulled back his shoulder, cast, waited a moment, and made his forward cast far to midstream.

We had been driving with the windows up to keep out the driving wet. Now we got out of the car.

A storm of smell came down and smote the face, the whole body, entered the clothes, the ears, the sleeves, invaded. From the bridge itself, up the hill, the whole town, streets, sidewalks, all, was covered and painted with manure of cattle. It lay fresh beneath our feet, trampled out by hoofs and boots, a rich shine under the rain; as far as the road rose before us, up to the tower now glistening blue in the wet morning.

The speakers were turned off. The sound that buzzed and increased and fused with the smell, that sound was of bursts of shouting and curses, long harangues of refusals. The sound of bargaining, a beating noise of demand and counter-demand. The cattle fair had begun before dawn, and was going full blast; spread slippery under all, stable-muck laid on thick, and shining. Cattle-filth up the whole length of the slippery hill, not only underfoot where it was visible, but up the whole height of the air. It was palpable; it was what we breathed; it was the air; it was time and the present.

A moment of quiet, as if a conversation between giants had paused. Near us, as we put our feet down slowly, not to slip, please not to slip, near us the certain and lovely sound of a violin. A man was playing in the middle of the street. Somehow the black cattle parted for him, as he climbed the hill making music. He walked with his jaw down on the instrument, his eyes shut, walking slowly, playing a fine thread of structured music, sure notes passing up and down the rungs of form. He walked with his violin and his hypnotized look, the shit spattering out as his feet came down. Behind him his companion, with a shock of hair standing straight up and the drops of dew balanced on his head. The companion held out his cap; he was necessary to the music, a part of it, not making music but making their presence possible. He followed behind, with spatters up to the knees of his trousers; the man ahead playing and playing; now it was not so much form, nor notes passing; squeaky and comforting the strange sounds went by. It was a fiddle, not a violin, a homemade instrument with well-carved vents and a straight body, no slowly molded and Italian shape. The musician carried a cigarette between the first and second fingers of his bow hand; his collar was open, and his lapel was dog-eared and furred with mist.

The music went up the hill, clear, soprano; and the muck spurted out under the fiddler's boot. Up he went. I gave him a coin with a salmon on it. Up, he lost himself in the crowd beneath the tower. High up there in the blue-and-white square of lines and the flags, there is the white Puck, an effigy blurred by mist, ankle-deep in his food.

Now the shouting came up again and swallowed the music. The man beating the cattle with his stick, whacking it down hard on a hipbone. "I'll turn yer cap around and turn it back for ye! Fifty pound for a three-year bullock, yer stone mad." They were at each other's throats. The third man, the middleman of these bargaining, came out from among the men watching, spat, volunteered his services as agent, waded in and broke them apart, and the process of the deal went on. "Eighty!" the first yelled. "I'll have eighty!" and the other raised his stick in rage.

My friends were walking ahead of me. It was too slick, and I lacked confidence; I planted one foot before another, and felt the clench of my teeth. One foot slipped, cutting a stroke like a child's finger painting. Another wave of stench met us; it was real and brown, a sonority of booming smell. Suddenly the entire feeling of the scene changed with that reinforcement of the smell. The hill, the town, became so intensely what it was—a cattle-market that was one root of the Fair, without which there would be no Fair—that the black cows and bulls, the unshipped, plastered, overspread excrement became itself: part of whatever was unfolding, part of whatever was being bargained for. It may have been the man with the cap walking with the inexorable musician that said it to me first. The money walking behind the music, the listeners able to deal with the man walking behind the fiddler, a tinker who had made his own instrument and his own music.

The place changed. It was producing a smell that was not only bearable, but right, appropriate. Ah, but the slippery, treacherous, sliding hill of it. That threatened me. At this moment I knew that my knees had been shaking for some time. My feet refused the move. I had done this before, once over air high up in the bleachers of a ball park; once on Baldface, far up the granite wall, with Emerald Pool lying below and hidden, my green and secret rushing cleanly water; once in Spain, when the firing began again, in Catalonia, the first night of the war.

Nicholas was speaking to me. "Do you want to buy a pair of Wellingtons?" But I could see at the street corner a girl in delicate shoes with high and lovely heels, stepping among the dung, picking her way, seeming to choose among many subtle possibilities. I shook my head. I could walk now. Liadain, who had said nothing but had turned to me, began to climb the hill again.

3

"WALK sidelong," said Nicholas, "crabwise. You won't slip."

We edged up and over the Square, among the drovers bargaining and the black herds. I turned to have a moment without the sensation of beginning to slide, and rested facing downhill as I had when I used to climb, summers, in the White Mountains. Down the hill came two men with lettered banners speaking of help for the families of the I. R. A. prisoners. They walked steadily and straight up the hill toward us.

"Recruiting, more likely," said Nicholas harshly. "They recruit at these places. Do you know Stephen MacBride," he asked me, "Maud Gonne's son?" He did not wait for me to answer No. "We know them in our group in Dublin," he went on. "We had a West Indian—a lot of them come here to learn guerrilla warfare from the I.R.A.—He came to us, in great conflict, and he worked with us until—it was a victory—he spoke up at a meeting in Dublin, and renounced assassination as a method.

"O they get lots of people," he went on. "There was a South African boy who wanted to set a date on which the houseboys would poison their masters. He wanted the reservoirs poisoned."

"But what Ireland owes the I.R.A. can never—" said Chris.

"Even the goat up there," Nicholas cried out, waving his long arm. "He's male, yes, he's father, he's king, but he's England, too..."

"...For whom many Irish have volunteered and died, darling," said Liadain. "And many starved without volunteering."

"They've hated and loved England," Nicholas said between his teeth. "They play their hatred out."

I thought of Frances Wickes, the analyst, looking out at Monadnock, among her work and her writing, saying to me, "The greatest task of our age is the introversion of war."

Chris was leading; he had an idea, and we headed for Cahill's, diagonally across the street, past the troops of black cattle, their heads all pointed away from the center of the road, their drovers dark-faced in anger and hope of closing their deals, the middlemen patting them, turning their heads from side to side to follow the match, patting their other, turning back.

The pub was half full of drovers and cattlemen. Four of them were arguing at the bar, their dark drinks before them. At a corner table a thick man slept, his head down on his arm. Beside him sat a man who stared and never moved; every line in his scored face made a mask of loss. In the far corner, a man talked to himself, muttering numbers: orange bony face, opaque yellow-red hair, he looked like Van Gogh disguised in drink.

Two tinker children came to the door and asked for money. Peter Cahill came over, greeted us, and took our order. His face was gray. He glanced at the children; his eyes moved slowly, they wanted to close. "Easy touches," he said; "if you give them money, they know that's what you are. Word gets around, then they're all here at my doorway.—Noreen's just gone up to get her four hours.... I? No," he said, and grinned, "I always count on losing about a stone every Puck." He patted his flat stomach. "It's better than dieting, isn't that right?"

On the floor and the stairway, broken glass, rocking puddles of beer half-blotted by sawdust, and the boots of the cattlemen stippled. Into the stink and shavings where we sat drinking Guinness and mineral orange ventured a young boy, child-faced, shallow-featured. He was wearing a green sweater ragged and gone at the elbows. Eyes very proud. He stood in the doorway, another boy and a little girl behind him. The boy in the green sweater went over to Peter. "Can I sing for all?" he asked.

"Sing away," said Peter, his own voice almost lost in hoarseness and weariness.

The boy stood in the middle of the floor. His lifted voice climbed higher than sound, cloud, fiddle music—true and alone on the slender treble, the words

Que Sera Sera

and singing on, filling in the words I knew well; and then departing from them, he was making them up when he lost them, singing for his own luck and chance, his high reed of a voice singing, the holes at his elbows mouth-shaped in his green sweater, his mouth singing

What will be, will be

—a dice-player who casts and casts, trying for his fortune and always coming up with the same fate; asking his mother and her womb, asking the clouds and the weather, the way the birds fly, anything; the men in their stupor, the glaze-faced man and the man asleep, What will become of me, and getting forever the one answer

Que Sera Sera

The glaze-face shook his head. The words of the old play, cloud-storming Marlowe, came back to me, and Nicholas said them then:

What doctrine call you this, Che Sera, Sera,
What will be, shall be?

Outside, the mist was steady. The manure seemed to spread further and thicker as we walked. The King on the tower, as we came close to the base, shook his head; his bells rang; and he looked down on us as we turned up our faces in the laden air. It seemed impossible that he should be in the same position in which he had stood at the crowning. He did not appear to be constrained, but born to stand there. He was white and cleanly. His look came straight down to us from those light eyes. His look shed down upon this morning something of great assurance, something smiling and durable. The filth lay over the whole world of Killorglin, on us and under us, and his look rained down.

"Don't you hate it? Isn't it unbearable?" Liadain asked.

"No, I really don't. It isn't." She was behind me now, and I waited on the downhill slope. Downhill was not so good. As I started again, I slipped, this time with both feet. She caught my arm. We laughed. Her hand was slender, strong, I could feel each finger rooted deep in the fine hand.

"I thought when I first got it from the bridge, 'She won't be able to stand it. She's American, after all.'"

I looked at her, but I had to watch my feet as I placed them slowly on the sliding downhill way.

"Well," said Liadain, "I've lived in a farmyard, but that was nothing like this—a whole hill, a whole town, and you—" She stopped short. I felt her slip, and supported her, but I was sliding and trembling.

I'll tell you, I said, and thought of the pleasure of having this all in its fullness, open, for once. I remember the Day of the Dead in Mexico and the happiness and relief it was to me to have death dealt with openly, in bones and boneyards, sugar skulls, picnics with tequila poured on the graves, the eating of death and acknowledgment, not pumpkins and spooks at Hallowe'en at home.

I thought of the story the Indian woman told me on Vancouver Island—Did you ever see a woman split down the middle? No, I said. I have; she was standing in what we call the community house, and everyone came in and she stood there and said in the strong voice, Won't somebody come and kill me? A shudder of shock and release went through me. This is the thing one is never supposed to say. Then, said the Indian woman, the shaman came into the house, he walked forward with the obsidian knife gleaming black in his hand and he said I will—and drew his sharp knife hard down her front till the blood spilled on the ground. He held the entrails up. We all saw them. Then we left the house.

Next day we came back. We stood in our places around the big room. There was the woman who was killed. She was wearing the evergreen leaves at her temples; she danced the dance of rebirth.

What was it? I said.

Some of us knew—the old people, and some of the others of us knew, that there was a young dead seal under her robe—when he did that, she was wearing a young dead seal. But it was for the sake of the second day. For the dance of rebirth.

When I first heard that, I told them, I remember the shudder of shock and release that went through me. "I still feel it. I was brought up not to talk about three things: sex and money and death. And the excrement, the wet and dirty—you know how they work on our cities to keep them dry? to try to display life as *not* sticky, *not* wet? I don't know why this should do—"

Liadain looked at her husband. He was watching me with a sardonic rictus; not a smile at all. He said to Liadain, "You know stables—"

She broke in. "Nothing like this. I think I mind it more than she does."

Nicholas looked past me then, intently, and I turned. It was the horse-dealer.

"'Morning," said O'Connor. He smiled, showing his split

teeth. High on his cheekbone, the mark of a blow was a dark raspberry color. "Missed you at the dancing last night." He looked strongly corded, rested, and natty in his green-and-tan worsted suit. He carried the slender stick of the market men, even though he had "no interest in cattle," he said. He had bought his ten horses and slept for an hour in the lorry. His blue flat eyes tried to say to Liadain and me what he had done before and after that, and was looking for now. He slapped at his leg with the slender stick, and showed his stained teeth again.

"Bit of an argument?" said Nicholas.

"I don't get into arguments," O'Connor answered. "I get into fights."

"The cattle on this side"—Liadain broke in, on a breath—"are they another breed? Why are they without horns?"

"O they're all Kerry cattle right enough," said O'Connor. He said "Kelly" for the county. "They dehorn them. Saw their horns off. They ship easier that way." He stepped sideways, forward, wanting to drive himself as a wedge between Liadain and Nicholas.

"Your business is done, then?" asked Nicholas. There was an edge in his voice and jaw. The smoothness, built of many experiences, of his professional life, had changed to a saw-blade, even in his voice.

"Business!" O'Connor answered, mocking. "I get that over and done with first of all. If you mean am I leaving, no I am not. You'll be around, this night?" he asked us; but his shoulder was toward me, he was speaking to Liadain. "I'll find you then," he went on before she spoke. A black cow went by, lurching and mooing, the bawling voice drowning out what Liadain said. Good-byes went around. The cow bawled again, a stick laid across her ribs. Nicholas was silent.

Going downhill, the barefoot children in the shit, laughing pure, running the slithery tilt of the hill.

I felt it on the backs of my legs. Walking uncertainly, I said to myself, heel down firm. A panic of slipping gripped me; I stood still, and the panic rose. You go ahead, I told the Hilliards. I'll come after, and meet you at the car. Chris looked down at my feet. "I'll walk with you," he said, and took my arm. I froze, unable to walk. Day of the Dead indeed! I thought, joy and release is it! and put my foot down slowly, gained an inch, and slipped. Chris pressed my arm and side; he braced me as if I were an extension of himself.

I was wearing open-toed shoes, bought in New York. Don't look at your feet. If you set your feet down slowly, I thought, you need not slip.

The beaten cattle, lowing beside me, nudged me with their horn-robbed heads. I slipped.

4

THE BIG and handsome tinker of last night was watching me, standing below me, on the bridge. Not smiling. Watching.

From a doorway where a woman stood shouting orders, singing orders back into the house, a boy brought a bucket of water, rocking the water over the wooden edge onto the filth, splashing fore and aft. The woman pointed in a great down-diving gesture of her hand; and the boy threw the bucketful along the arc she made. A strong arch of water flew out and fell flat, blue and white, washing a path through the muck. "Fetch another bucket then!" she sang. Six head of cattle came trampling through, black legs over the slight clean mark. The path closed.

Out of the Railway Hotel, the one place in Killorglin—6 rooms, B. & B. 12/6—a commotion in the darkness and a knot of men spilled out surrounding DISABLED FROM BIRTH. He was flailing his arms on the losing end of a fight. He tried to push his way back into the hotel, but somebody straight-armed him, and on the steps he lost his footing, slid and fell still sliding in the filth. A tall spare man picked him up, caught him by the shoulders and half-tossed, half-bowled him halfway across the street. DISABLED FROM BIRTH picked himself up to a sitting position, and sat there like a huge child, legs stuck out straight before him, shaking his big head with distaste. He struggled to his feet. He was drunk enough, but of sound body. His tongue was contained in his mouth; he was no different from the rest of us, not noticeably. He came back to the Railway door, wanting more fight. The spare man was waiting for him, his head on one side, balancing neatly on the balls of his feet. He brought one ferocious uppercut from the filth up to the underjaw of DISABLED FROM BIRTH. The man went unconscious before he reached the filth and lay spread-eagled in it.

I stood still, wanting to be out of it, not wanting to take another step and slip again. Chris gleamed happily at the scene; he grinned at me in quick pleasure. In the doorway across the street, the woman still stood, and the boy stopped watching and threw forth from his worn bucket another brilliant arch of water, a flat spill flowing downhill at the woman's feet. She nodded her head at me, in that easy gesture of greeting.

The drizzle had stopped. Bright blue emerging all over the sky. Sun striking the water and the filth; both glittered.

The sunlight on the woman's face. She was looking up at the dark part of the sky. "I hate to see the clouds topping the mountains," she said to me. "The rain'll come down."

Two tinker children came up to us as we picked our way slowly down the last block to the bridge. "Coppah? Coppah?" the older one cried, on two close notes of music.

"If you give them anything, you'll come home naked," said Chris. They came after us, coppah, and circled around us, coppah. I gave them their coins, the beautiful copper coins in my pocket, the bird and her brood, the sow and farrow, and the hieratic diving heron.

Mr. Regan, too, the victualer, was standing in his doorway. He saw what I was doing, walking with my slow unsure strange gait on the shining copper street, giving out copper coins, and his fine fat face reddened with the effort not to smile. "'Morning," I said, "I'm taking it slow."

"God and Mary to you," he answered. "That I see."

"Is it a good Puck?" I answered, teetering against Chris, and introduced him.

"That it is," said Regan. "Last night was very good. Everyone's come to me for crubeens; there are periwinkles by the thousands eaten with pints; and the lovely little plaster plaques of goats going just splendid; and the market today is not so badly too." He twinkled. "Sixty pound for an incalf cow, seventy for bullocks, and a little white-headed bullock calf of mine went for thirty-seven." He looked at me. "You know, I've been thinking about you and your talk of high places. You know who I hope you see? Father Quinlan."

My left foot slipped. Chris halted, and we stopped again, opposite Regan. "I'd like to," I told him.

"No good trying to find him today, of course; he's off somewhere." The broad face lit red. "You won't find a guard or a man of God in this gathering." The roar of bargaining rose behind us. "But they'll turn up again before it's over. You'll see."

"Slán agat," I said to him, slipping a bit, and so did Chris, a muscle of iron beside me.

"Safe home," he answered, ruddy, and he laughed.

I was on the bridge, very grateful for the flatness of it. The tinker had gone; the Hilliards were across the bridge, standing beside the green car. Partly dry, the stone across the Laune, just streaks and wheel ruts of dried brown tracked over its length, crossing, parallel, straight, like a sepia drawing of a railroad yard. The one fisherman stood like enchantment below, in the bright green reeds at the river edge, waiting for his strike. And across the Laune, the endless line of painted caravans: light blue, light green, dark green, pink, gold.

"Some people care only about cleanliness," Liadain was saying. "God knows what they think it's next to."

"That's a swipe at me," said Nicholas. "She takes all of that as English." The tinker children ran up to us, the same children who found us on the hill. They called "coppah?" and then, recognizing me, stopped short, hesitated, touched their temples in greeting, and went away. Nicholas leaned on his elbows on the bridge-wall. I was glad to be finished and on firm ground. I leaned there too, stretching my arms forward in the sun, the river repeating its endless syllables in varying, in combining, in ever saying, beneath us. The sun in Nicholas's eyes threw sparks of water-brown, clear, ironic. He nodded toward the line of caravans.

"Gypsies," he said. "All of them; Freud has them down. He says they correspond to something in us, and are the sign of that element in our society."

All right, I thought. They correspond to something in me.

He was going on. "Parasites," he said. "They are, in society, parasites. As much as any parasite that feeds in our own body. Irresponsible, ungiving, unproducing...."

"They give me," I said.

"O come on," said Nicholas. "You don't mean that; you're not sentimental. They speak for one thing only."

"What's that one thing?" I asked.

"You know, perfectly well. Irresponsible, unwilling, preying on those who carry their share of the work—The death wish."

"The death wish!" I repeated. "But what they give us when we think of them... I know the kind of hatred. The towns don't know how to feel when they see them... jealousy, longing, despisal. Do they wish to climb on them? We have gypsies in America. We have Negroes, brave, long-suffering beyond belief, controlled somehow in an insane situation. And the tribes, tribes of Indians cut off from the ways and still aware of tribe. As these tinkers, even when they put cars before the caravans instead of horses, even when it's plastics and not tin... They still have their signs, their patterans, a broken branch by the road, a sign of leaves and ashes, a way they are . . . " He was looking at me with contempt. I stopped, not wanting to argue; these are my new friends, I thought.

"Death!" said Liadain. "Like your woman," she said to me, "on Vancouver Island—'Won't somebody come and kill me?'—"

"The theory—" Nicholas began, in a patient schoolroom voice.

Liadain stood up from the wall. "I like that dance at Vancouver," she went on. "I don't think the death wish—Isn't it more like that? A lazy way of talking about the wish for rebirth? Couldn't it be that? . . . Tinker or not," she said, and walked off the bridge. "Chris," she called down to him. "What are you doing?"

He looked up from below the bridge. He looked into my eyes for the first time. "Bringing grass," he said, "to wipe our shoes."

5

WE SAT on the gray stone wall of the bridge, still looking at the line of caravans. "Or might it not be like *Waiting for Godot*?" I asked Nicholas as he wiped my ankles and my shoes.

"Might what?"

"Many people have talked about that as a suicidal play. It's very clearly not. It's altogether Irish, isn't it? Look: they talk about suicide a great deal, talk about hanging themselves—remember? it will give you an erection; if I only had a rope—" Nicholas nodded, and looked in my eyes.

"They long for a rope. Well, during about half the action of the play, there *is* a rope onstage—a long, fine, strong, new-looking rope. The rope that connects Pozzo and Lucky. A lot of the time, that rope is stretched clear across the front of the stage. All that time, nobody mentions suicide or thinks of wanting a rope. As soon as it's gone, they begin again."

"O come on!" he said again. He threw back his head and laughed, not the male laugh of yesterday, but the sneering tone that had this morning almost obliterated his attractiveness.

"And I suppose the I.R.A. are parasites, like the tinkers? Rebels and renegades, who will not face responsibility?" asked Liadain, and her eyes went yellow as she prodded him.

"Hostile, and renegade—useless in this period," Nicholas said.

"I know they're not what they were, but I'm for them—again, for what they remind us of," I told him.

"Yes. I saw you give them something in the muck. That won't ever see the 'families of prisoners.'" Nicholas mocked me.

"That's all right," I said. "I'm drawn to them. They remind me. Can you not repeat this, if I tell you a story? It's Paul's, Paul Rotha's, and he's going to make a film of it—a short, say twenty minutes, perhaps less. Anyway, it musn't be told. Unless you know it; it's a Dublin story.

"There's a block in Dublin, a slum block that was far behind in rent. The landlord hit on a plan to make money out of that block, tear down the buildings and put up something that would really pay, a bus terminal or a taxpayer—one-story shops. It would be easy enough to turn out the tenants: they were all three or four months behind.

"Word of this got to the I.R.A. And, one afternoon, two men in trench coats, with their hats pulled down—so—over their eyes, and one of them with a notebook, went around, knocking at every door, and asking how much rent was owed, in pounds, shillings, and pence—writing it down in the notebook.

"That night the Bank of Ireland was robbed, of the exact amount. Next afternoon, the tenants in the block sent for the landlord's agent. They had their rent, and wanted to pay up. He came at once, and went to every door, and collected everywhere; gave them all receipts. The only thing was that on his way back to his office he was waylaid in the street by a couple of men; and that night the exact amount that had been stolen from the Bank of Ireland—pounds, shillings, and pence—was returned."

As we sat there, laughing and smoking, the big tinker walked toward us. He stooped in the roadside, and the long curved muscles in his back pulled against his jacket. He had bent to the grass, a place blackened by a tinker's cookfire. He leaned over the dead embers; the set of his head was that of a man reading. There were stones among the ashes.

He walked to where we sat.

"Do they tell you something? The stones?" I asked.

"Yes," he said. "It is a patteran; it gives me a sign. Sometimes leaves, sometimes branches, sometimes stones. One family has already moved on. This tells us where."

"And where have they gone?" asked Nicholas.

"If you care to know—to the Crescent at Tralee, what the Rilantu, the Irish, call the Bull Ring."

"It seems to be a tinker's fair—as if it used to belong to your people," I said.

"Not belong, I don't sang," he answered me. "But we traveling folk belong to it by right. Even the gaverog on the tower, we somehow belong to him. But the town has taken over, and no more, no more, for us. The day will come, next year, the year after, when you'll see the signs up: NO TRAVELING PEOPLE."

"How would you have the Fair?" asked Nicholas curtly.

"If I had my n'ok?" he answered, with longing. His face shone, dark, strong, reinless. "Many things." He looked at me without looking at my face. "Not that kind of dancing. Boxing, I would have, they'd have a ring squared off. And no more goat, not tied by the feet like a spanceled horse—or a housewoman."

"Or a king," said Nicholas, and took out his pipe and pouch.

"I'd have regard for horses, not let the horse-torturers in," the man went on. "And let them be faithful as we are faithful, or be kissed our kiss for the faithless—bite their tongue out. And marry as we marry. Jump the budget, we say; that's jump the great leap over the barrel together. But part if love sickens and dies."

"Have some tobacco?" Nicholas offered his pouch, and the tinker took out a pipe from his jacket and accurately, with delicacy, shook the tobacco in.

When we walked to the car, we saw that the filth had spread to this side, too, and the bargainers were swearing in the road. Nicholas took off his boots and shut the trunk of the car on them. Liadain and I sat in back, and Chris from his front seat turned.

"No more slipping," he said, and winked.

"*You* know," said Nicholas, clenched around the pipe. "You know the fear of slipping."

"It didn't really—outside of that—bother your American sensibilities?" asked little Chris. Nicholas turned slightly and answered for me, in his slightly rasping, reassuring voice. "Appears not," he said.

6

RIDING away from town in rainy noon, we opened the windows of the car. The last brown smell of the Fair blew out and backwards on cool flights of air. In flowed the breath of roadside, of all fields beyond the field of filth and shouting; the scent of shrub keen on the air clearing now of rain, even under the sparkling dripping trees. We turned with the road to the right, leaving the river, and saw the mountains before us, in the perfumed country. The noon was heaped with lovely gusts: a breeze ran over the little vivid stream we crossed, and these yellow flowers everywhere, and the hay stacked there waiting to be saved as we speeded past the empty road toward Carrantuohill, to the cloud streaming and perfumed over his dark head. On the mountain's right, a bright less lordly mountain breathing a fine smell of clarity and silence, and nearer us, a cone-shaped, smaller mountain, a foothill even more still. The earth opened its direct and tender scents and smells and silences.

A yellow house as we passed sent up a sigh of turf-smoke, its rich odor of warmth bending to us in the breeze like a touch, grateful to the nostrils in the cleanliness of the sky. We drove past the last farms and entered the black-brown plain, where turf and turf-cutters are all the crop. Harvesters, their gestures of leaning on the narrow blade, the aromatic fern-forests are made into essential fern in turf, essential scent in the perfume of myrtle.

Two women biking home, with long easy pedaling. One in a blue coat billowing past the back wheels, the other in a green tweed suit; they waved as we overtook them and went on. It may have been their waving, their stilled faces seen for a moment, the thrust of their pedaled rhythm, that gave them the look of being for the time fulfilled.

Liadain beside me smoothed her subtle orange-and-yellow skirt. Nicholas must have felt her do that, seen her from the corner of his mirror, heard somehow the skirt under her hand. He looked straight ahead, and I could not tell what he saw. The glass of the car gave him sight forward and back, windshield of perception, mirror of memory, and it was very tense between him and his wife. He knew, as the married know.

"How was it for you in the streets, my dear?" he asked her. And, mock-solicitous, "What did they do to you?"

"Well now, there was a bit of pinching and poking," she said, melodious Irish for him.

"You liked it," said Nicholas.

"I didn't look back," said she, and her breast rose and fell. "I was afraid of slipping in the muck."

"Aha!" said he. I waited for the discovery, but he gripped the steering-wheel and said nothing. The peaks of the mountains above us were taller. Our way dipped and rose over the soft bog, like a road that breathes.

"There!" Chris spoke. "You can see—over there—the Peak of

the Sheep, and the five peaks of Cruach, the Reek. They are, and I give them to you in English, the Cliff of the Crows, the Rough Flagstone, the Yellow Little Bold Hill, Windy Gap, and last, the Cliff of the Goats. And then, behind, Hag's Glen, and—" he pointed— "the Devil's Ladder still out of sight."

"You had a grand time last night, didn't you, Chris?" Liadain asked. "It's strong in you, coming back to Kerry?"

"I enjoy," he said. "Let me stretch my leg, Nick, will you. I've got a kink in it."

Over and under went the road in the soft country, among the softest soundless scents of open summer. Brown country giving way to pink; bog, turf, to stone. The crossroads, empty; and a turn to where the foothills come down to stony farms, deep green and outcrop.

"I heard that a man was arrested last night," said Chris.

"Two," answered Nicholas, biting the empty pipe.

"With the police vanished?" I asked.

"For housebreaking. Two different houses. And that was only because they were caught, in the houses, and turned in—What's that?"

For a moment, I had seen it too. A flock of whiteness as we turned into a cool shadowy curve in the road, among trees, and higher, the white, on the sloping fields of the lower mountains.

"Looked like goats!" Chris cried out. "But I am goat-haunted," he said happily, ruefully.

"Sheep, I suppose," Liadain said, craning around.

"Awfully hard to tell them apart." Nicholas took his pipe from his mouth, put it in his pocket, and pulled a deep breath. He looked like a man about to quote from the *Britannica.* "The ruminant of the genus Capra, closely allied to the sheep... has for all time been regarded as the emblem of everything that is evil, in contradistinction to the sheep, which is the symbol of excellence and purity—"

Liadain hooted. "Their *all time*—how long is that?"

"Separate the sheep from the goats—what's that?" I asked, and heard my voice, very stupid.

"It *is* hard to distinguish, particularly in Ireland," Nicholas said. He had his quoting voice again. "Certain hair breeds of sheep are, to the layman, only distinguishable from goats by the direction of the tail, upward in goats, downward in sheep."

Over our laughter, there was a rushing of water, a changing, combining sound in many voices, in a single voice. We turned to the right and over a bridge. One way to Glencar, the other to Glenbeigh; rock-rushing waters, mountain-sprung and violet in their speed, white, eddying, dark-halted, full of choices.

"We almost stayed at the Glencar Hotel," said Nicholas. He looked around at me as we came to the lake. "We would have missed you altogether."

"You would have missed the Fair," said Liadain. "You almost did, anyway."

"Glencar," said Chris. "What is that in, *Lickeen*?"

Where the wandering water gushes
From the hills above Glen-Car,

"How does it go, then?"

In pools among the rushes
That scarce could bathe a star—

He said the line again. "What does that mean?"

Liadain laughed. "Not large enough, of course." She looked out her window. "The sallies around the lake, I love them. Willows," she translated.

The glittering cold water we had passed went through my eyes, brown, black, and glittering past stones; and the short, black-muzzled donkeys cropping near the road, and the great wide sun-blue lake. Sleep, I thought; and may have slept for a moment.

"A.E.?" Nicholas was asking.

"No, it must be Yeats. Very early," Liadain said. I went deep asleep, again for just a moment, for when I opened my eyes the lake and its sallies were still on my right.

"What I want to know about is the two-legged Puck," Nicholas was saying. "I suppose that's one reason why I'm doing what I am."

"And it is difficult here?" I asked out of sleep.

"In Kerry?" He snorted. "In Dublin, then? Well, the most difficult thing is—"

I waited.

"The fact that Freud was a Jew."

"I know one Jew they accept," I said, but he was talking without hearing.

"They can't accept that," he said over my words.

"That's one reason, of course, why Hanaghan is so valuable. He is trying to make a brotherhood, a group without a name, a city of man."

"And Jung?" I asked.

"Jung they consider ratted." He looked in the mirror and our eyes met. "You can see that in the correspondence, if you don't think so. But he did, really. Of course you can make psychoanalysis popular if you leave out childhood sexuality. Hanaghan is making a religious bridge for Freud. Actually, the Church is beginning to follow him. And Jung has helped, just here; the Dominicans having followed Jung, things are giving way.

"Sometimes priests will talk to a patient—not tell anyone to go to an analyst, but say to a patient, ask him, 'Is he doing you good, do you think?' and go along when the answer is 'Yes.'"

"Of course we accept a Jew," Liadain said to me.

"You almost did, didn't you, darling?" Nicholas asked her, with a curious edge in his voice.

"O, Morris—" said Liadain. "But I left him for you."

"Morris?" echoed Chris. "What about him?"

"He's a Jew," Nicholas said.

"Yes, but he's an Irishman," said Chris.

"Tell her what the children say. . . ." Nicholas prompted.

Liadain smoothed her skirt of the "Irish mixture."

"My two oldest made a rhyme," she said, "not without help, you know. And all the rest have picked it up and they sing it out to me:

She might have done a Morris dance,
Worn ruby rings and lived in France—
She might have gone a jig a jog
Down the wrong road to the synagogue.

But that's enough of that."

"There's feeling in many directions," said Chris. "What about the sign as you come into Bandon—

TURK, JEW, INFIDEL OR ATHEIST,
ALL ARE WELCOME HERE, SAVE ONLY PAPIST—

Wasn't there something about goats? And Morris?"

"During the war," said Nicholas. "A rumor. I hardly believe that one. They did say, during the war, he bought up goats in the hedgerows and sold them to the English for sausages."

"That's out of character for him," said Liadain.

We passed a tall stone by the roadside, a stone marked and scored with parallel lines, half-lines.

"Do you know those?" Liadain asked me. "The Ogham stones, and that language?" She showed me Ogham, with its one-to-five count, on the fingers, for letters. She told me of the stones scored along their edge in Ogham.

She told me of the great buried monument far out the northern peninsula—the right leg, looking out to sea from Killorglin—the tall stones and the fallen pillar near Dingle, covered with cups and circles, the ruined dolmen, all seeming to be parts of a great connected constellation—something like Stonehenge?—called The Gates of Glory. And the languages of the vagrants of Ireland, the crumb-foxes without rights, except that in ancient Irish Law "freedom" and "holiness" were synonymous terms, and an unfree man was Untouchable. In the wanderings and the famines, bands were on the roads, protecting themselves by any means, including their language, thieves' jargon, like Negro slang in America which has passed into white language and is written down. These tongues—Shelta, The Masons' Language, and the others, that have nothing to do with the vagrants or with a craft: Bog-Latin, Hisperic, and all the Oghams, have come down to us, from stones, theology, the vernacular poets, and the slum taverns of Liverpool where, in 1890, John Sampson learned Shelta and wrote it down.

She told of the early Ogham stones later carved with the Chi-Rho cross and spiral and the inscriptions in boustrephedon, as the ox plows, one line left to right and the next line right to left.

"It's somehow very easy to read," she said.

"*Very* easy," I agreed. "*The Reader's Digest*, even, tried it on a page a few years ago."

"That's adapting," she said. "We have the old limitations on art, made by Gregory the Great, limiting the symbols—that gave us our vines and decorations on the Celtic cross."

I'll show you a game of limited symbols, I told her. She gave me paper from her bag, she had a sheet of watercolor paper. Using my pen that jiggled in the little car now racing along a river, I showed her the game that Berenson's secretary had got from him and taught me. It is an expressive game, and the pictures you make are based on these four figures: a square, a circle, a triangle and a squiggle.

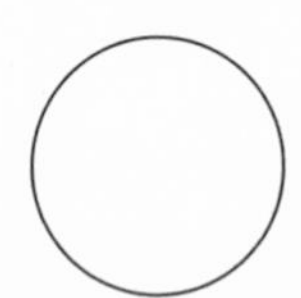
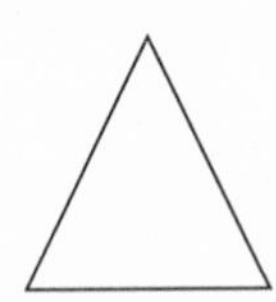

Then you tell the players: Make a drawing, using these four elements in any way you want, on any scale, just so long as each touches at least one other—touches in any way, inside, outside, at any point. Of course it can touch more than one other, but it must touch one.

Liadain drew, with the circle dominating, touching them all, surrounding. Now, I told her, these are the meanings assigned to the figures.

"Literal meanings?" asked Nicholas, dashed.

Not narrow literals, I told him. He wanted to draw. So did Chris. We were within sight of a long bridge across this wide river, the Behy.

They made their drawings. Nicholas did not want to show his, and asked for the interpretation.

The order in which you have drawn the four symbols is important, I told them. Remembering the order, this is how they go: the square signifies order, form, literally the house. The circle stands for love. The triangle is energy, ambition. The squiggle is freedom.

"Look what I've done!" said Chris to Nicholas. He glanced at it, and started the car.

"You know," said Liadain. "'The wandering water gushes'—I don't think that's *this* Glencar at all. And here is what follows: 'Come away, O human child!'"

We crossed the last bridge, and came to Glenbeigh and the Inn.

7

THE COOL, clear bath, not deep enough, with a thin wafer of lemon soap. The linoleum floor. And then cool, bathed dark sleep.

They were all in the dining room, at separate tables.

Nicholas came along the hall, and stood with me. "I've been savage all day, I know," he said.

I waited for him to go on.

"The Fair is getting me down," he said. "I won't go back to it. But I know you want to, or have to, or whatever—I'll drive you back to Killorglin."

"Thank you. Yes, I want to go all through it, the three days."

"Later this afternoon then?"

We went in.

8

AS I WENT into that room, I dove deep. I could hear the talk and the thrush-song outside, the taffeta movement in the hydrangea bushes, the distant clatter of the one palm tree, sound of tropical arithmetic. But the focus had changed: I knew isolation. I dive into myself, everything is water-green and sonorous, for a moment I have the same surround that I knew long ago, when in San Francisco I entered the many-storied echoing structure of glass and water-music, the Sutro Baths.

Although here at these tables are the Hilliards and Chris talking, and there the English family, there a film director, there the gynecologist and his wife, eating their sea trout and salmon.

To go far into the loneliness, having come halfway around the world, to remember again the fear of death, madness standing on the threshold, speechlessness coming along my throat while I wait, while I too late approach action. And the balls of the goat, the great horns, the aura of the King—he is far, he is away, chained high on his blue tower.

Where are the Hilliards taking me? In their cross-talk, building up their own slender tower. I remember, again in San Francisco, the pale blonde drink, and as I drank, seeing beyond the edge-lit rim of my glass the stone fact, sexual, penetrating, welcoming, the linked organs declaring to me . . . well? Linkage, collision, those principles that Eisenstein calls the ways of making film. Classicism, romanticism; *lingam* and *yoni*. However, the stone must transform; both must become fire; both must become flesh. Here we begin.

All right, then. What have we done, on the second day?

Have we turned into our opposites?

The quarrel between the Hilliards is banter, far away in a green, water-and-air fusion of echoes. Chris is looking into my eyes. What if it were Chris, if his look, just now, took hold and acted the hero? He looks away. He would have to; I am locked into whatever happened to me when I walked down this hall, into this room that is a great echoing cavern that is myself.

A curious movement of "deepening" is going on.

The whole scene becoming a world entire, a romantic who considers annihilation, some dreaming Alexander who must conquer himself or go mad—not "conquer" the world or himself, that is the madness, but move as a man approaches dread Everest, makes peace with the dread white forces, prays, climbs, swears and goes, breathless, unable to think of words, dragging this foot, that foot, and bleeding, his head a world and populated by visions, his heavy feet two worlds, into the winds and freezing plume of crystals: his hands are planets, and he goes. Climb and be with the forces.

What are they saying? Nicholas: "Spenser among the streams of Buttevant, alders whispering, the bathing places . . ."

Chris: "Spenser! He wanted all cattle marked, sold in the open market. Cattle—our chief currency."

I fade out on the talk. Something is happening to me; as if I were at a play that I fully accept. I do not identify with the heroine. I do not identify with the hero, or the murdered father, or the lustful mother who marries the new king. I identify with the whole play.

Over my shoulder, I hear dialogue:—Are you a dualist?—I don't think duels prove anything.

The scene before me falls into fragments.

In the doorway, the Green Queen is standing, without her robes. Without her crown, of course, which was given, and is on the horns of the King.

"Kathleen!" says one of the waiters, who is her father. I get up and go over to her. Wait a moment, I tell her. I have wanted to speak to her, and I go down the hall. One moment, and she waits for me. I open my suitcase in the room with its cabinets and its peat fire laid again for the night to come. I feel my camera; I have not taken it out in Ireland. And I bring it to her in the hall.

It seems an unlikely gift for her, but her face lights. "I always wanted one," she said. "I'll take it with me this afternoon to Fursey's Well." Or did she say "Percy's Well?" What is it? I thought. I know nothing of this country. But she was smiling, the Green Queen, in the full look of a child.

Her father beyond her stared at me in my madness. It was on his face—crazy American tourist—as he looked at the camera. He began a question, let go of it, dismissed the matter with a few words, and we walked toward the door. I stopped at the entrance to the bar, and they went into the sunlight on the road. Someone was calling my name.

It was thick at the bar. Unreal density of these words. I fought to hear, still in my green-water state, the smoke sliding past me in currents. Nicholas was saying to me, "And you think you can bring in movie people! Or what? Write about it? The love, the shouting, the frustration? The sordid commercial breakdown of an ancient wildness?"

What did I answer him? No, I thought. I can do nothing with it, nothing with my own storm of feeling, or my speechlessness. Or my own desire that looks at him, looks at Chris, looks at the wife of the gynecologist with her well-cut cheeks, opening her mouth for another drink of Power's down the bar.

What is the meaning of "Liadain"?

"What does 'Liadain'—What is that name?" I asked.

Nicholas hooted. He took my arm. "I'm driving her down to

Knocknadober," he said. "Do you want to go to the Stream of Chastisement?" I had no idea what he was talking about; the words fell away as I heard them. I am the stream of chastisement, I thought, seeing his fierce eyes and his thin-carved mouth, the long body flowing away. I shook my head. I would go "for a walk." She was going to the high dark hill, down the road away from Cahirciveen with her husband; they walked in their rhythm to the little Morris car; and across the road from them the Green Queen and her father talked. The little girl held up the camera and called to me. Her words were lost in the wind of a truck passing. The truck slowed beyond them, stopped, and backed slowly to pick up the girl. The truckful of children shouted, pulled the girl up along the tailgate, and the truck and the car went off to Knocknadober.

The grinding of the truck awakened an old echo: the trucks of my childhood, when it was the building of New York in which my father's whole public life was maintained, the sand and gravel and stone which would be poured out into the roads and bridges and the city—more and more a poured city, rising glassy over the water. Voices of the old wars and love, the boys of the dark entrance-halls, the ferocious magnificent music, and through all roads, the slowly spinning bodies of the trucks as they rolled, mixing the concrete on their way. Wetness—the mixture of those buildings and of my family's pride.

I turned and walked the other way. One after another, the clear field-life swam into my sight: this yellow weed, a black cow. The road I took was toward Killorglin, and toward some kind of death. Clouds swam down to my face, full of isolation. A fragment of blackness, rags of mortal horror, a mixed dark howling. Words of Stobaeus crept out of the pace of my going: "The mind is affected and agitated in death, just as it is in initiation into the mysteries, and word answers to word, as well as thing to thing; for to die, to be initiated, is the same...."

It was my death I was facing, through weakness, through inability to act, through ignorance. I was completely inadequate to deal with what was going through me. I could not even see these people clearly, or hear the words they were saying to me.

I was at the river. The Behy rushed white along the gray road, throwing the banks into fierce yellow-green, throwing the black rocks toward the strength of death and life. Under the arches of the bridge, the river, fast carrying all the notes and words together.

A woman who had left the bar as I came in was standing beside the road, brush in her hand, laying-on gray. The work on an easel there was the scene before us: the stone wall along the road rushed as fiercely away from us as the river came toward our place, and far at the bridge crowded the shapes of houses. Everything broken into itself by the fresh force of water. But that force was the same as the force of the road, the green, dim purple force of the horizon mountains.

Eileen Costello talked to me as she worked. She asked me questions about America: What really happened to Dylan Thomas? What does Jackson Pollock mean to painters now?

A car came toward us over the bridge, and stopped. It was little Slattery and Mary Antrim, more red-boiled sunburned than before. Yes, they had gone to Killorglin, but how could I bear it? They hadn't got out of the car, and they could smell it still. They had gone on at once to Killarney. As magic as they knew it would be, and by boat to Innisfallen.

Did you see the Sky-Woman? asked Eileen Costello.

They did not know what that was, they said, and after a little, drove away.

What is that?

The Sky-Woman of Kerry, the *Speirban*. She is poetry, said Eileen. Her statue stands there, but you look for it. It carries the names of the dead Kerry poets, Pierce Ferriter—hanged where the statue is; Geoffrey O'Donoghue, ruined by Cromwell; Owen Roe; and Egan O'Rahilly, the poet of the *aisling*, the dream vision. "Brightness of brightness," said Eileen.

She worked for a while, and I sat on the stone wall. The river.

She talked of the great games of today. Not only Puck, she said. St. Lawrence Day on the highest place in Wiltshire. And I thought, on Sunday when the Puck was crowned—they're running the Palio in Siena this moment.

Why don't you live in one of the cottages? she asked me.

Who is Percy? Or Fursey? I asked her.

The Percys we know, but that's England, she said, working on opaque white sky in her painting. Fursey, that's here. Our saint of visions, she said. His spring is on Knocknadober.

He's an old saint, you can find him in Bede, I think. Beehive cells, monasteries, ecstasies. Around 648, his year is. But his visions are the great ones; Dante knew them. Some of the ragings of demons and angels, and the rescue of souls from the flame. But one is sharper than the rest.

Saint Fursey on high, and earth far below him a dark valley. Despair, gloom on earth, and around him in the air four streaming flames, fires kindled separate in the four directions.

One to burn the souls of those forsworn and untruthful.

Two, to burn those given up to greed.

Three, those who stir up strife and discord.

Four, those who find it no crime to deceive the helpless.

Then the fires swept together; they coalesced, and threatened him. Fursey cried out. A voice answered him; the angel said, "That which you did not kindle shall not burn within you." Fursey drew breath, and a great voice could be heard, saying *Respice mundum.*

The scene lightened around me; the gray changed, the greens, the purples, the yellow weed flamed up. I stayed there a long time. Nicholas came by; we watched the painting grow. She finished, and put up another board. Take it, she said, handing the painting to me. It's only a sketch.

Come and paint the Spanish boat in the harbor, I thought, and said so. I might, in about three weeks, she answered.

In Nicholas' car—What's Liadain? I asked.

You have no right to speak of Kerry and not know, he said, in a generous rasping voice, and told me. That is the name of the great woman-poet of Kerry.

And Fursey?

Fursey's the vision-man. Torn in two by love of mankind, driving him to active work, and love of solitude, driving him to his hermit's cell. That's his holy well they've gone to: the Stream of Chastisement. Up Knocknadober.

I thought of the goat standing high over Kerry, the four flags flapping at the cardinal points. And the great rushing halted. The light and the world were clear. I came back into them.

9

"I'LL DRIVE you in," he said. And turned the car—"I'm beginning to be fond of these ferryings between the Inn and Killorglin. . . . What does Killorglin mean, do you think?"

"Church of Lawrence, the guidebook says," I answered.

"D. H. Lawrence, too, I imagine. Not Lawrence of Arabia."

"It is my father's name," I heard myself slowly say.

"And will you phone him when you phone your friend, who is going to China? And send him word from Puck?"

"He died this spring," I told him.

"Hah!" said Nicholas. "And the Puck reminds you, then, also of him?"

"Perhaps he does. I know that when I saw his legs were tied—My father died with his feet gone, of gangrene."

"But King, power, giver," Nicholas said on a deep note.

"He died—both his children disinherited. For disobedience."

We drove in silence. Finally Nicholas asked me whether Liadain had said anything about the Fair to me. She had not. "We're not going back to it," he said. "It's been a day at cross purposes."

"And let the morning be the last you see of it?"

He did not answer, again. When we were near the town, he began to tell me of the book he was deep in: Jones' essays, the one on war. "Everything he says of war echoes this fair to me. He shows how war, as a massive social contact, creates none of the impulses; it only releases them by affording a certain sanction to them." He said the book compared peace with monogamy, "which, Jones says, society accepts in theory, but never in practice." He spoke of the attraction of horrors, the deep appetite for horrors, and the homosexual desire to be in close relation with masses of men. "You know what he says war does?" Nicholas continued, "it brings man a little closer to the realities of existence, destroying shams and remoulding values. I translate that, I keep translating to the Fair."

"I'd like to read that."

"Would you? I'll leave it at your door tonight—before you come back. He doesn't leave it at that; he goes back to the origins, psychological origins mainly in relation to one's parents—actually, feelings about the self, the mother, and the father—the last probably least."

We were at the green fence again.

"I'll be fine here," I said. I looked at him hard. "What bothers you?" I asked him. "Is it the filth and the evil?"

He grinned his glaring grin. "I knew a man—a friend of mine sold his soul to Aleister Crowley," he answered.

"You're sure?" I asked. "You know He who loses his soul... You have to have a soul before you can lose it. Or give it away. Or sell it."

He set the brake, and looked at me with the narrow look, the look with which he had begun. He smiled a wide smile, the smile of yesterday. Something had given way.

"Tell you what—we'll all meet at ten tonight, shall we? Where?"

"In the Square," I said, getting out.

"I'll find you," he said, made his U-turn at the crossing, and was gone down the road back to the Inn.

The town was washed clean, swept clean. The colored bulbs were on in daylight, the white Puck stood aloft, brooding, gentle, hardly moving. At the foot of the tower, a man was speaking into the system, offering chances on a raffle whose first prize was a trip to Lourdes or £60. The drawing would take place at the church tonight at 9:30. The second prize was a trip to Lourdes or £30. The third prize was £10. The fourth prize—I never heard that, for the music began above the calling voice. They were playing arias from Italian operas. In the lull of an aria, I heard the voice again—"And the drawing will take place tonight at the sound of the drum."

Four abreast, the Yanks came by; I could spot them by their narrow ties. And Sergeant Nolan came running a few steps out of the barracks door, stopped, puzzled. I was facing him, and he looking at me, bemused, and doing the classic thing: scratching his head. "It can't be!" he said, without knowing anyone was standing in front of him. But many were, and I among them. The dancing was beginning, and I moved with it until we were within reach.

"Ne faydir shin!" he exclaimed. "That is impossible!" and turned and went clattering upstairs to his apartment. He came down again with a dark vivid blue-and-green blanket. "I'm troubled about the blanket, even," he said, directly to me. "It's her best blanket, from Sneem. Well!" he added, in a distracted way, and called over his shoulder. "Looby!"

Guard Looby came out at once. "Wouldn't that vex a saint!" said Looby. He saw Sergeant Nolan looking at the blanket. "She won't grudge it you," said Looby.

Sergeant Nolan looked up at me. "You won't credit this," he said. "Come along, Looby." And to me again, "There's a sort of a sea-monster in the shallow waves, at Inch, and we'll be going down there in the hack." With the blanket all plaid of blue and green and black, they made their way down the side street, against the tide that was streaming in to dance. The music changed to "Because You Come to Me."

Mrs. Nolan put her head out the window. "Nolan!" she called, with the music, but it was no good. She saw me. "My Sneem blanket!" she wailed at me, and laughed at once. "You know what for? Some creature on the strand." And pulled in her head.

"What's that?" asked the sandwich woman. She'd been selling until 6:30 this morning, and had just begun again.

Now I could not bear not talking to Ella another minute. When I left London, she had been getting ready to go to China, seething with excitement, nerves, dread overwhelmed by eagerness. I had driven with her to the airport once—Idlewild. She was seething in the charming, fiery bewildering way of hers. Looked at the airlines clerk with her long Egyptian eyes, and seethed at him. But he was impenetrable—"Madam," he said, in a voice to cool the Gulf Stream— "You have a *minute* and a *half.*" She was flying to Peking, and we had said our good-bye, and I had asked for Chinese poems, and word of Chinese science. "Chinese science," I could hear them sneering in America; "there is no Chinese science," as the owl in the book, with the boy standing before him, closes his eyes and says, "There is no boy."

The public phone in Killorglin is in the Post Office. The phone and the Post Office are half the shop, the long desk and the booth all down one side. The other side has a counter, and sells sandwiches and buns, fruit, cigarettes. Mr. Connery, the journalist, was in the phone booth, which was marked OUT OF ORDER. He was phoning his story in to the Dublin *Times*—KING P-U-C-K, he was spelling out, "K for Kevin . . . was the best Puck Fair ever for the business. . . ." The booth was freshly painted, sticky white, shiny dry black. I went back to the man at the switchboard, the Postmaster, and placed my person-to-person call to London. The Postmaster was just going home. "But the call!" The call would go through, operator or no operator. Clear orange stained glass, the window seen from inside the dark shop, with Players Please lettering very black and backwards. Green lime Woodbine sign, lettering white. Dark blue stripe at the top of the window. Donkey outside braying between orange shafts. Torn red-and-white poster remnants behind him. And through the window, the black-gray silhouette of a girl in a shawl, her red fine hair surrounding the silhouette of her head. Clear fluid cigarette smoke the only transparent thing in the gathering dark.

I could hear Connery, going on with his story: "...and overflowed into the adjoining streets. Full stop. The usual concertizing..." He came out finally and saw me. "You've been waiting all this time!" he said with double sadness. "Ah! If I only had a typewriter!"

"No typewriter!"

"There's none in the town," he said. "Owen Cross, at Valentia, has one. Well, now. There's girls go up to Dublin for a typist course and come back, and there's no machine, if they did get work."

The bell was ringing for my call. As I went into the booth, "Mind the paint!" called Connery. A knotty, gnarled man came in as he left. My call was going through, and I faced the corner, where the OUT OF ORDER sign stood upright and authoritative.

Ella's voice, full, mocking, thrilling, happy, was there in its immediacy. "Well!" she said, inches away. "Are you still a virgin?

"I have your letter," she said. "It smells and shines of sea and sun and the hills and the goat.... I wish I were there. We'll do it sometime. Only now I couldn't get both into my spirit, West to the ancient and East to the new!"

I let the gnarled man into the booth, and bought a pack of Woodbines. He had placed his call long before, I could hear him talking to the Dublin operator, and still his party did not answer. She would call him again in an hour. He came out.

"Couldn't help hearing you," he said. "China! China, coming into Killorglin!" He asked me to have tea with him, and we went back to the corner shop. The tower was playing the "Donkey Serenade."

"You like to see the old woman t'ilin," said the tea-shop woman. "Thousands of ham sandwiches at sevenpence, you think. All right!" and brought us tea and sandwiches.

Tom Crimmins, the gnarley man, had come back to Ireland. He had told his sister in Dublin that he would be home the next day after thirty-eight years in the States. He had been the youngest boy at the Post Office, in the Easter battle after long training, and there he had been shot in the foot; and somehow had got away, and hidden out in an empty house for two days, praying that his dog, his setter beside him, would not bark. At last he had been captured, though, and had stood it all, and been let off from the firing squad only because he was so young. And after that there was nothing much for him, with his smashed foot—he still wore a special shoe—nothing but the Tara brooch that Countess Markiewicz gave him, and which I could see in the Dublin Museum whenever I reached Dublin—and that I must do. But young Crimmins had got away on a forged passport, and reached New York, and been an elevator-boy in the old McAlpin until he got a job with the United Fruit Company, and went then to the Caribbean, and later to the Northwest, and found the girl he married, and stayed there till she died. Now he had shipped back, landed at Cobh, and come straight here last night. Why? Because it had been banned the year he left, and it had gone on anyhow. Nobody could enforce that ban. Puck had been going on for a thousand years, maybe five thousand years. But a Black and Tan had leveled his rifle during this illegal assembly, and had shot Puck dead, on his throne. Tom Crimmins had heard the skin was kept, somewhere in Killorglin.

"The name," I said, "I've heard it as Church of Lawrence. Is it that?"

"The feast of St. Lawrence is on the tenth of August," said Tom Crimmins, "but Killorglin is Cell Forgla—and Forgla means choice."

Mr. O'Sullivan would know about the skin of the Puck. I took Tom Crimmins to his bar, and we drank with him while Grania went upstairs and brought it down. "Ah, the dust on it!" she said, and showed us the bullet hole.

It was time for the phone call to his sister to go through, and Tom Crimmins went back to the Post Office and the sticky phone booth marked OUT OF ORDER.

In from Killarney with all her cups and plates, said a tea-shop girl, work, wash up and work again, it's worth it.

The striped booths, the darts game, the Bingo cloths marked off on the street. The ring-toss trundled in again, with the crib beside it and the baby asleep beneath the flares. The man under the cart being asked a question: "I don't know, ask the woman upstairs." And Mrs. Shaughnessy, the tinker woman, saying to me, "Tell your fortune, love? Don't say 'Later' any more. I like your face, love. Could you just give me those grand blue beads at your neck; bluer than anything in the world, anything on the land and charming me? Shall we lush a glass of ale together? Well, then, your fortune, with four large coins in your hand, held tight."

10

AND OVER the river, blue caravans, with cream-color doors. We walked there, and little Mary Filomena was sitting on the caravan steps. I went into the pink world inside, all designed tightly like a ship's cabin; and we went along the line, with its goats, cropping at the edge of the Laune, its black-and-white, well-cared-for horses, the naked babies squatting at the puddles, the ornate round gilded decorations at the tops of the gold pillars of their homes.

The rain set in again. I had tea out of the copper kettle in the pink cabin, under a pink ceiling, and set out into the rainy dark, the high squealing sexual laughter at the bridge, the heavy wordless sounds, hot dogs in the Square, the goat snug and dry under his own roof. The pipers were again in the Square, skirling and excitement in the chest, along the ribs, in the rain. They were heading for the Oisin dance hall, and the drawing for the raffle had begun. Many barefoot children following the pipers. Many children, and many men.

The Hilliards and Chris were in the Square, and we went down the row of pubs. They kept on their mackintoshes; we did not stay long at each place, and talked desultorily, they of where they had been, of the "awayness" of the north (said Chris, cocking his head and eyebrows), of "lonesome and isolated Achill" (said Liadain, who was dissolving, changing). I told them of the "sea monster" ("a shark, I think" said Nicholas).

Then we turned into one of the pubs in that street, roaring, streaked with shouting, overhung in smoke, and pushed our way in to the back room. It had an earth floor, its walls were painted dark red, thick red daub. A wooden staircase went up over the smoke. An unpainted door was slightly open on the black rainy night behind the room. It was one of the best places I have ever walked into.

Out of everything of the second day, music, singing, this ring of people. There were perhaps fifteen of us, and we were there for each other. The two men who were at the center of all were—what? a tinker, a Spanish gypsy? he was all dark, olive and black with light green eyes; and his friend was thick, tan and orange and was playing the harmonica without pause, and dancing a hornpipe and somersaulting as he played, never taking it from his mouth, somersaulting with a collected, strong will, bunching himself and circling over himself while the gypsy played the banjo, played and played as we fell into the music, dove into it, bathed, swam.

I looked away at the people along my wall. I was sitting on a long table, delighted with everything that was in the room. When I looked back, a young fair man, bull-necked, with a searching face like a young playwright I know, was singing "The Boys of County Armagh":

The ashes of Brian Boru.

In the warm, smoky room, a hoarse woman followed him, rolling as she sat, drunkenly calling for a song farther back. "'Rose of Picardy,' let's have the roses," she sang out, and drew us back to our birth, before, to deaths and mourning we never knew, long-drawn-out sighs, cries, keening, roses.

"I'm going out back," said Chris, and opened the door. In the long black view, there were the fair-grounds far away, their points of light in single stars, stars, galaxies out there. Rain puddles on the ground with constellations in them. Sky cleared, black, stars over stars.

Chris came back. "I'm willing to dance," he crowed, charming and offering. And there he was, stiff to the knees, holding his arms stiffly at his sides, and dancing as if every wildness in him existed between his knees and the ground. Hornpipe, step dance, the language known to Kerry and that room; how they clapped!

Nicholas they passed by, friendly and understanding; he could stay, and smile, and not be called on, not for a thing but for his delight. I cannot sing, not in this room, but I can say:

> *Dusk is drawn and the Green Man's thorn*
> *Is wreathed in rings of fog. . . .*

Liadain is next, and she rises curved like the figures carved with the curve of ivory, those women whose hips curve true like the tusks that were their ivory. She is slender, she is in the music, and changed: girl, mother, poet, and she is singing a song they well know, with old postures and inflections that speak straight to them all:

> *. . . For the girl I love was beautiful I'd have you all to know,*
> *And I met her in the garden where the praties grow.*

She was the garden, she was the "Grecian bend," she was the "jail," she was the children, "girls just like their mother and a boy the image of me" who would be trained.

For to dig out in the garden where the praties grow.

She turned to Nicholas as the clapping rose around her, in so extreme a sweetness, and walked to him, staying close to him as the next singer began "The Homes of Donegal."

We were in the car again, again on the road back.

Liadain beside me was singing, her voice high, high, tenuous silver, through the smoke of night and drink, the song of the clear black night, singing . . . a young lad . . . singing "She Moved Through the Fair."

My young love said to me: "My mother won't mind,
And my father won't slight you for your lack of kind."
And she stepped away from me and this she did say:
"It will not be long, love, till next market day."

She stepped away from me and she went thro' the fair,
And fondly I watched her move here and move there,
And then she went homeward with one star awake,
As the swan in the evening moves over the lake.

Last night she came to me, she came softly in,
So softly she came that her feet made no din,
And she laid her hand on me, and this did she say,
"It will not be long, love, till our wedding day."

In my room at the Inn—ghost! I thought, alone. Puca is ghost, they have taught me, pocan is he-goat. Jonah, really not for me, grieving over his unfinished play and his unfinished wife, run off in a burlesque of a tragedy with a Kinsey operator who was his friend; I wishing only to act out my love, my wedding undone, my child two-thirds the world away, almost as far as that China of unbelief to which Ella was flying.

A knock at the door. Nicholas with a book.

I met him in the whispering late night. "Jones—you've brought your book."

He gave it to me. "It's not Jones, it's my master Hanaghan."

Deep night. I write to my son. I start to write to that friend who sent me here: "Mixed—in a tragic penetrating beauty, music and filth, cattle and drunkenness, the gypsies and the goat and the marvelous..." I let it be there, unfinished too. Where is the real desire? Among the stars, the constellations, of desire, all approached in me, all unfinished, unbegun now in this quiet. This moment which is the only moment, the present, with the rout of the past all there, in love, in touching, in violation, in sorting out, in arrival.

A great cry in the night startles the pen from my hand.

A glass rings in the cabinet of silver.

A cry from Paxos, I think, that the sailors heard, calling "Great Pan is dead!" Cry I have always known, looking into the dead eyes of the living, of the death-drawn I have loved, that cry heard and never till now asked. Who cried out? Whose voice was it, crying news? The first news ever known by me, and I was four and told to beat a drum up Broadway—it was false news, the false armistice. I know this well, this is false news too, piercing thousands of seas and the waves of time.

Who cried out?

A cry answering a cry.

Sleep, and forgotten dreams.

SCATTERING DAY

1

A BOOK, a blue book, a book of substance, good to hold; a book stamped in gold, on the front cover the head of a girl holding up an open book, her hair parted in the middle and opening in wide gold folds, like a book.

I open at random. He says, "European man declares his deceit and snobbery in his houses, their arrangement and decorations. Their fronts are often artistically decorated whilst the backs are barbaric. Take a walk down your back lanes and look at your houses from the rear and you will be looking into the European soul." He talks about the abruptness of difference between front and back.

He tests his insight not by what the European says, but by what he has achieved. His cities, says this man, writing a plain and burly English, declare not the fellowship of man but the disparity of men. They declare man's mercilessness as much as they declare his mercy.

He goes on to the defense of the city. The armed forces and diplomatic services, he says, "reveal his denial of the fellowship of man and his assertion of the disparity of men. They also uncover the dark secrecies of his heart."

He speaks of the cries: the trained cry of the choir, begging in its music for mercy. But stranger lamentations: the needy in the slums; the girl waiting for a baby without a father, and her tears; the smirk of the pervert hunting for kin; the suicide muttering as he knots his cord to the lavatory beam. Wordless cries, of those who will hang by the neck; the insane locked in their hospitals, "bound by physical, chemical or neuron-severed straitjackets. We dare not look into their eyes of terror or madness: we dare not meet the possessed spirit face to face."

The agony of man, he says, is the revelation of his spirit. Would you know man? Look at his city.

2

HE SPEAKS of another cry. This is a cry that has been spoken of as helpless, but it is full of power. It is the infant cry, the birth-cry. Hanaghan says, "It is the most profound and powerful force in nature." He gives it to me in this book, crying across life to something dormant in the father and mother. It is the rousing, the haunting; this cry seeks out the tingling of the nipple, the tone wakes the parental need to help and protect, to relate the crier to his surround and to let him go; it cries, across years, to their feeding his mind, to their watching his loves, to their learning to let him slip from them, newly built, the ship. The cry is self-preservation; the cry matures the woman and the man, and may make them parents.

3

"THE ARMED forces and the diplomatic service," Hanaghan says, "should be held in high regard. What do I mean? I shall tell you. Some persons, more than others, bear the cross of our unresolved hatreds and in-turnings; these have far stronger sadistic impulses than others and to them is given the hard task of self-mastery. A number of them unload their sadism on their neighbors; becoming bullies, criminals, destructive mass-leaders, or cynical critics. Others, with difficulty binding their hostile impulses, find their sublimation in offering to defend their city or fatherland. These are the true professional soldiers, sailors, airmen, policemen and diplomats. Instead of making cruelty, or killing, their aim, they offer to be cruelly treated or killed, if necessary, for the sake of their people and their nation. That is why they are worthy of honor. Though they may kill, killing is not their aim; they surrender their private sadisms—which often are very intense—in order to serve and defend society. Their aim is the defense of their fatherland, even unto death. This willingness is symbolized in the beautiful uniform they wear and in the glamour and glory that gathers around them. I do not want to dull that splendor or pale a glory that truly is theirs. They are equal to us all: they are superior to most of us in that they have striven to socialize those impulses, reserving their destructiveness for the defense of their people and their fatherland.

"Nevertheless, we must not fail to read the meaning of the armed forces and diplomacy. They concrete and incarnate the evil in our hearts, whose harvest is disease, famine and death and the destruction of the city. They declare unto all that man the creator of the city is also its destroyer."

4

I SLEPT; and while I slept, the book rested on me, open. I turned and woke; the book slipped from me as I lay on the low couch. It turned and opened to another place. Trust the moment, I thought; read here; and I read:

"I had an interesting insight given me about this a number of years ago when in London." Turning the pages backward to find out what *this* was, I went through Hanaghan's setting-forth of the choice before each of us: whether to go ahead with evolution itself, or whether to turn our libido to devolution, away from the life task: to bind ourselves to ever widening circles of interest by the bonds of love.

The story he told was of a woman who was a patient of Jung's, and who, during her training to be an analytic psychologist, had been encouraged by Jung to work out her anal fantasies plastically. Hanaghan spoke of her as "a very refined artistic lady," and as I began to see his curve of meaning, I read this literally, each word flat. He said this lady had power in sculpture, and she had been modeling animals, "all most faithfully constructed with accurate anatomical knowledge and sense of poise and movement. They all were full of grace and rhythm. They had a chaste classical Greek clarity and harmony. But in each of them there was a distortion that startled me as if I had been suddenly slapped in the face. The anus of each animal was formed into enlarged out-growing shapes that were grotesque; fannings, curvings, over-curlings, cuppings. There was no end to them." He realized suddenly what these signals were: everything was emphasizing a secret meaning. Hanaghan writes that he wants to use this art to answer his own question, and this is the question. "Supposing that the reversal of the self-preservation instinct, together with the regression of the sexual libido to oral-sadism, could cause structural changes in human beings, what structural changes would we expect to see?"

Through that lady's art, Hanaghan reached his view of nature. "I believe," he writes, "that all creatures of prey have partly abandoned their evolutional task. First halting, and then becoming fixated at the oral-sadistic level—the first level of invasion of the body by the spirit—they have withdrawn thereunto their forth-flowering love and interest." He speaks of the spider, whom we understand; the wolf, the bison, Blake's tiger, all of whom we understand through ourselves. He remembers what James Ward, at Cambridge, said of the beetle—a beetle suffers all a beetle can suffer when he is trodden upon.

But there is a difference between the human fixation and the animal fixation. We express these changes symbolically; no actual change of structure, with us, occurs. But in the animals, we know these heads, jaws, claws, and beaks; we know the Fall, not of man, but of Creation.

5

HANAGHAN says, in this book, which is not very large, this book which is rather thick, the deep-blue book which is sometimes poorly written, or rather not written but greatly spoken—he says against sects and creeds, "Man, not God, splinters humanity. . . .

"Let us for a while lay aside our housekeeping, our care of pigs and cattle, our solicitors' scripts and our barristers' briefs. Let us lay aside our doctors' appointments and our craftsmen's tasks, let us lay aside our psychoanalysis and our poetry. Let us enter into the Silences. Let us leave for a while the Create. Let us abide in the Uncreate."

6

THE GARDEN stretched outside, sunny, colored, various. My doors opened on it. I got up from the bed and went to the window, and opened the book again. Warmth from the garden entered the room; I want to read right through this to the end, I thought. But what end can be here? What is this saying to me? I stood in the doorway with brightness falling straight through onto my face and hands, onto my breasts and the book; I opened the book past that woman's unfolded hair right to the end, three pages before the end of that blue book. I started with the first word on the page:

"... Hero? How does the mystical search for sonship with God the Father become the search for sonship with a mythical king?

"Freud recognized this Myth. Otto Rank showed that it was a tale told not only in each infant-heart but in the folklore of all nations. At our mother's knee we have heard many a fairy tale dealing with this theme. But neither Freud nor Rank nor the folklorists understood its meaning, so it finally lost its significance. Why did Freud and Rank fail?

"In my opinion they failed because they were unable to transcend the biological concept of the self. Had they done so they would have recognized the Myth as an imaginative creation veiling a wish of the child-self to be loved beyond human loving and honored beyond all human honoring."

They would have seen the displacement and distortion of the content, he says. They would have seen them as due to adult human folly. "For the adult is more anxious than the infant to mask the Myth's inner meaning."

He speaks of Anna Freud's warning against *ad hoc* translation of symbols. It is not that the king and queen are symbols of the parents.

7

"LEAVING the theoretical child of discussion," Hanaghan goes on, and asks you to consider your own childhood.

"If you could relive your infant days of loneliness and disillusion you would find that your deepest being cried out for someone more trustworthy than your parents. But to whom did you cry?

You would find that you turned to someone whom your parents looked up to and trusted. Why? *Because it is a law of our being and therefore a law written in the heart of every child, that we cannot go from person to person as one goes over the stepping stones of a river. Love must go before us and lead us. We can only go from one loved person to another that is loved and honored by that person. We can only desert our parents by turning to those they honor and love, unless we react entirely against them and even then the connection is there."*

Who is the unseen father, asks Hanaghan. Someone whom your parents honor: "only on to such can you pour your withdrawn libido and being. This is the law. But whom did your parents honor? . . ."

Reverberation of the question. A tide among the flowers, up through the hills, sonorities.

8

NICHOLAS at the door. "Reading it, are you? You might like to see him. Big-headed, very much a man, too much man for some people; big-headed Jonathan. Beethoven-headed.... And what do you make of the book's name?"

Society, Evolution & Revelation.

Come back to Killorglin, now, he said. Liadain's on the big hill, sketching. Chris won't budge; no more, he says. But we'll be glad to go with you to Valentia, after.

After the end of Puck Fair.

9

NICHOLAS and I drove into Killorglin. He talked about Hanaghan, how the book had been made out of talks that could hardly be conveyed on the page. He stopped at the Post Office; he wanted to call Dublin, where three patients were in emergency; and he wanted to speak to Hanaghan.

"I'll go ahead," I told him. "I want to read that book at Valentia, and the bulb in my room is just strong enough to throw a reflection on the window at night."

"My calls are going to take longer than that," he said.

"And I want to see the Nolans." We would meet at the hardware shop. There was at least an hour before the Puck would be brought down.

The Square was less crowded than it had been at any time since I first saw it. The booths were clearly visible; I could hear the loud ticking of the Wheel of Fortune, and the man with the white rats running on his chest could be seen as he squirmed in a kind of medieval squirming and knotting, and suddenly threw his leg up and over his shoulders in an ancient angle. A woman was standing beside me, and as he thrust his foot behind his neck, she cackled.

"Is it really the Day of the Children?" I asked her.

"It is not," she said, with the air of one answering a superstition. "They did use to say that the children took over from the fellow up there, but there is little heed we take for such lies for Yanks and tourists.

"If I had a cup of tea now, I would drink it."

"I regret it, but I must be moving now," I said to her.

"What hurry are you in? It is early in the day yet. Stay and drink a cup of tea here with me."

"No, thank you, as I must visit the Nolans, and my friend will be anxious about me if I am so late."

"O, that is the way with the men always, God help them."

The Nolans' stairs were familiar now. I rang their bell; I was curious about the call from Inch.

The door burst open, and Sergeant Nolan stood there. He was rumpled in his uniform, he had not shaved, his patient, corrugated face was that of a man who had seen a miracle. Who was seeing a miracle, and had come away for a moment to answer the doorbell.

"Yeea!" he said. "Come in then and see him!"

I was aware of the knot of men at the door, of the packed stairway, of the men in the hall ahead of me; and I had learned a phrase or two of Irish.

"Rud airh bi oonthuch err shool?" I asked him, and knew the answer. "Anything wonderful on?"

He took me by the arm, and steered me through them all to the bathroom door.

Where yesterday the tub had been full of the children's clothes, socks and underwear making a foam on the waves of laundry, there lay a dolphin in the bathtub, tail up among the faucets, head down and now submerged. He was wrapped in the Sneem blanket, wet and comfortable around him, and Guard Looby was scratching his stomach while he smiled the smile of the sea.

"We had him in a cell downstairs," said Nolan, "but it was not possible. Not even when the blanket was thoroughly soaked. So we brought him up here."

The phone call had come when the grownups on the strand at Inch could stand it no longer. Every time they drove the "sea-creature" away, he returned. He had made repeated efforts to leave the sea, in order to play with the children on the beach. The phone call had said that the children were frightened. They were, indeed, all crying when Nolan and Looby arrived; but it was Nolan's opinion that they had begun to mourn only when they understood that the grownups were having their creature removed. Repeatedly, the grownups had put it back in the water. Repeatedly, and smiling, the dolphin had returned.

Nolan and Looby flung the blanket out over him; and, more through his willingness to stay near the children than through any skill of theirs, he had let himself be taken prisoner. In the hack on the way to Killorglin, he had seemed discouraged, and once, in the cell, had grown faint for a few minutes. But from about four in the morning on, he had been fine in the tub.

There was a hooting outside. "Looby!" commanded Nolan. "Tobin!" Together, they lifted the dolphin, Sneem blanket and all; we pressed back to let them pass, and they went halting down the stairs, Nolan commanding. From the hall window, I could see the smile wide and curling and the blue-and-green of the blanket slowly enter the hack. "Take them to Waterville!" said Nolan. The hack slowly made its way through the people on the street.

All the Nolan children were around me, warm, miracle-struck. Mrs. Nolan was in the hall, mopping the floor. "Let them be bringing my blanket back, that's all!" she said to Nolan as he climbed the stairs in a storm of distinguished feelings. Some of them concerned dolphins.

I went down the left side of the Square to the hardware shop. There was a smell of firelighters and oil, and a forest of paint, cardboard, stair-brushes. Farther in, there were stepladders, broom handles ranged in palisades, teapots on a perspective of shelves; cast iron pots and pans, stewpots, bean jars. The ceiling of the shop was packed thick with its own stalactites: tin cups, plastic overnight bags, walking sticks, and an enormous choice of vitreous enamel.

The owner looked and looked for a 100-watt bulb. Finally he came back to me and said, "I sold the last one ten minutes ago."

10

NICHOLAS beckoned me from the doorway. We went driving in search of a place he had heard about in Dublin. They used to crown the goat on a hill outside the town, he had been told; and we went down the road toward Desmond's Howl and Castlemaine.

"It must be along here somewhere," he said. We drove under trees to a clear place, and got out of the car, looking back toward

Killorglin. It was obvious that the countryside was flattening out, and that we were looking backward toward the only height, the town that dominated this landscape of green painted green, lit green.

He turned the car, and slowly went back to the bridge across the Laune. If I had the patience of that fisherman, I thought, to stand and cast again and again, like trying to write one thing all my life. It may be that, I thought. I could never tell any of this except in what I do, except in what I am, leaving something behind me like a patteran.

"That tree shape," Nicholas was saying, "that's high; not as high as the tower, of course. I wonder what Philip was talking about."

We parked, and began to walk up the hill, past the corner where yesterday the boy flung his arches of fresh water. Regan was standing in front of his shop. We asked if there was a library in town.

"O there's two!" he answered. "We're proud of that. One here, and one up the street and around to the left." Two! We stared at each other, and went in. He led us to the back of the shop, and there, on half a shelf, were the eleven books that made the Circulating Library, and beside the shelf was posted the list of books on the Index.

Nicholas told Regan what we were looking for. "O it's the history you want!" he said. "Then Father Quinlan is your authority." He pointed to the bench in front of his store. Three old men sat there, arguing; they stopped and waited for Nicholas to ask his question, and they deferred to the priest in the middle. He looked like an old memory to me, the memory of the idea I had had in my teens of a French Priest, learned, enormously experienced, with a vast face that grew as I stared like the faces of myth; a nose that was a map, warted, crossed-over, experienced as his eyes. But now the endless penetration of the eyes began. He was talking to us.

He told us of Conway, the Welshman with the beautiful

daughter, Avis, who married Blennerhassett; and how the town was dominated, and what became of the "carnal assembly" that was Puck Fair. I had not seen this priest before; the priests and the police were regaining their function, I thought. "There was a massacre here, where we talk," Father Quinlan was saying. "In those days this was the orchard, the square, where the goat stands"—we saw him, a stroke of white on his blue tower—"the square was the orchard of the castle, and the place was called Castle Conway. But that is what you want to be seeing, Castle Conway. The goat used to be set on the top of the castle tower, the highest place."

The town turned around my head. Castle, I thought in my confusion. There is no castle here, any more than there is a library.

"It's just a few steps down the street," Father Quinlan waved, with a slow, kind gesture, to the street before him. We swung around.

There was a bank at the corner, and behind the bank, a garden fenced-in. Nicholas, in the bank, spoke to the guardian, who jangled a bunch of keys, winked at us and said "O ay, I'll show you the Castle." He led us in the sunshine down the warm street to the iron gate, and lifted a heavy padlock. There were no words on the lock; only the numbers 333. The first key would not go in. I looked at the dense green ivy, the moss and grass within the gate. I heard the complaint of rust as the lock gave way, and the guardian opened the gate.

This was the place in the shape of a tree. From this garden, standing on this soft and springy turf, grown greener than anything beyond the walls, we could see the line of caravans beyond the river. Each round back of blue, gold, pink had the definition of objects seen in a *camera obscura*, sharp and deep in the live air. We walked a few steps in the hush of bees; the green seemed to soak its color from the air, leaving it clear, quiet, but indeed full of dialogue.

"You're standing over the wall," said the guardian then. "This is the Castle, at your feet. The Geraldines fought here, and the Templars. Their skeletons lie here, just under us—Lord knows how many, piled against the wall. They used to dig for them and find their bones. Chalk-white. Then they gave up digging."

An old boarded-up building faced us blindly, in back of the bank, invisible from the street. It was the old granary, built where the Castle was torn down. The last shell of Castle was here, a standing staircase overgrown, the windows out in its hollow overgrown with ivy and grass, ivy with sky clear and warm within the spaces of the leaves.

The guardian winked at us. He said, "I'll leave you be. Just pull the gate to when you leave—I'll lock up after a bit."

This was where the siege took place. Below my bones, the bones of the men heaped high, the great wounds gone.

11

HOT SUN, finding everything drenched and drowned, finding me and saving me, salvaging the hay spread out like pale hair over this county, piercing the gold and the throat. We went into the first pub for a glass of wine. On the right was a cool dim room with benches and kegs; on the left, walled-off, the bar L-shaped and crowded. A voice from the left as we came in called "Hilliard."

Nicholas swerved as he walked. I saw beyond him the man calling. He was sitting at the bar, his white face pointed at Nicholas in a large sensitive questing attitude; small mouth. He held his beer and nodded as we were introduced. It was Morris. Nicholas looked as though he had expected for years to see him now, this moment.

"Come to see the goat, Hilliard?"

"Why yes."

"I suppose you think the goat is a symbol?" He smiled and went on. "The goat's no symbol." He took a long drink of his beer, and looked closely at Nicholas' face.

"All those years," he said, flinging out the words. "What happened? Did you take orders?"

"I went into analysis," Nicholas said. His face was going white; the color climbed his forehead as I looked at him.

"Same thing," said Morris. "Just another church." His spread, sensitive face swung from one of us to the other. "Are you two married?"

I made a flat, side-to-side gesture with one hand, and the bartender brought us two glasses of wine before Nicholas answered. "I married Liadain," he said, and the white began to ebb in his face.

"You didn't!" said Morris. "That's terrific! You—and your verbal arabesques! An analyst. And Lia!" He began to talk about the Fair; he had just had his fortune told. "She said I'd rock the cradle for a son." He raised his head, very high, putting his small chin up. "I suppose you both, you each, have children." I nodded.

"F—" Nicholas began, and cut the word short. "Yes," he said.

"Well," said Morris belligerently, "I work with them. In films."

"No!" I said. "Of course—you made *Fais Dodo.*"

"Have you seen it?" he asked happily.

"Not yet," I told him. "But Paul Rotha's been talking about it to me."

"I saw him in Brussels," said Morris. "He told me a story about Capra there, and what Capra said about Jean Marais. Marais had just come from Japan, from shooting in a hospital where radiation patients were being treated, and Marais said—" He told us the acid story, and then broke in—"But I'm not living like that now. I'm traveling with the tinkers. I've been in a caravan for eight days, coming from Wicklow, and to run into this situation—no women for three days, that's what the Irish want—I've grown to hate a lot of things, including the combustion engine."

Nicholas, after a minute, said that we had been walking, and we left him on his stool and went around the thin partition.

On the other side, the big room was cooling, smelling of plaster and wine. We could not see the men on their stools, only the bartender and the end of the bar. We sipped the deep red wine, almost all shadow, hardly a red glint in this dim room. Nicholas began to relax; it was as if he remembered his whole life, and unwound.

The door of the pub opened, and two tinker women came in. One I had seen and spoken to, and she now had a baby on her left arm. The other was very young, and she had a little girl with her, the very little golden-haired Mary Filomena, who lived in the pink caravan. The young woman came forward toward me at once, to ask for money. The little girl hung behind. The woman with the baby started, more slowly, to advance toward Nicholas.

From around the end of the bar whipped the bartender. Just as the young tinker was asking me for coins—"or a ring or a bangle or a jewel for the neck, dear"—and as I opened my bag, the bartender closed in on her. She had not seen him head for us, and with a startled movement, swung away, hurrying for the door. Mary Filomena saw a scene of fear and pouncing, and reached for the full skirts of her mother. Just then the bartender overtook the woman.

The kick that he gave her struck through dress and flesh; through the muscle, I heard it knock fiercely against the bone of pelvis. The sound of the knock was loud, a ferocious broken noise with no overtone, as if wood fell on muffled wood. The tinker woman went down at once, spread on the floor in her full skirt, her strong legs out toward me in peninsulas, her little girl down beside her wailing; her coins scattered at one side.

I put my glass down on the barrel-top. The brute sound began again in me. I saw that Nicholas was standing, too; we were helping the woman to her feet, and gathering up the child, gathering up the coins. Nicholas put his arm through the woman's other arm, and we walked with her, half-lifting her along, I carrying

Mary Filomena, and the other woman running along beside us with her baby. We went down the street almost to the corner before we stopped.

"Are you going to be all right?" I asked the woman in a foolish voice. She was walking evenly. She put her hand to her hip as Nicholas and I let go. I stroked the little girl's hair.

"I'll sakel him!" she said, in bitterness, to herself and the sky. Then, "No," she said, "I'll be all right." She looked back at the pub door. "You didn't lush up your sridah—your wine," she said, in amazement.

"You don't think . . ." I started to ask Nicholas.

"Go back and pay?" he finished. "I wouldn't take a drink in his room." He spoke to me over the head of the woman. The children were comforted, we walked a way with the women, and they went down the hill to the bridge, slowly, but evenly.

12

THE CORNER we stood on, staring after them, was the one where we had been given tea before the Crowning. Through the curtained window now came the small strong crying of the newborn. Again, ineluctable, the cry: they speak of it as demanding, but it is not that. It is one of the most strongly evocative acts of life. One's wish to answer it is exactly equal to that power.

Nicholas stood fixed and listening. "That is within a day of the first cry," he said. "Hanaghan writes of it, in his book. It marks the making of us as parents."

We heard it once again. In mid-cry, it was answered. The sharpness broke, and a satisfied breathing entered into my own lungs and throat and face.

We stopped at a betting booth in the middle of the Square. Nicholas put a coin on a 2-to-1, and won. We both tried one, and lost. Then, in a burst of anger and gaming, I put some half crowns, the coins with the beautifully cut horse on their reverse, on the 8-to-1 chance. The wheel spun and spun, and came through for me. The man behind the counter began to pour half crowns in front of me. I did nothing, and Nicholas said, "No—take it and play half of it." I nodded, and began to play.

"You're a little odd about money," he said. "Where do you think it comes from?"

"At least I know where this comes from," I said. "It comes from my friend who left California for Europe early this summer and could not stay—who wanted me to have this. Who made it possible after Paul told me it existed."

"Thousands of people made it possible," he said. We went on playing.

Beside me stood a broad man who had come up to the booth just now. His skin was dotted with tiny blue or black spots, pricked out as if by powder burns. He waited until my play was finished, and then spoke, with great courtesy making his speech to us, thanking us as a tinker for leaving the pub when the tinkers were kicked. He walked uphill in the Square with us for a few paces, and then fell behind. We saw that other tinkers were looking at us as we walked.

Nolan rushed out of the barracks, and halted. "I told them Waterville!" he screamed. "They used their judgment, and took him to the strand at Glenbeigh.... Did you hear the phone?" he roared at us in a strangled voice. "Call from Inch, of course. Don't the damn fools know it's all Dingle Bay? Although I guess he could have found his way from Waterville, or Mallow. Or Spain.

"Where's that blanket now?" he shouted back into the building.

Paper, bits and lengths of colored paper and streamers, were all over the Square. The ground resembled a Jackson Pollock. Pink, green, white, some yellow, scattered—random, one might think at first, but then the laws of work were visible. Heapings near the booths and doorways. I remembered the tire tracks in the merde, and the things that seemed causeless yesterday—the drovers beating their cattle, the heavy, dull, merciless beating of sticks on Kerry cattle. The tinkers beating the small boys. The children crying in the mud down by the Laune; the children cuffed in the mud of the fairgrounds, near BIRDS ARE BEST; the children tagging along tear-streaked, late at night and far from lying down. Now the children began from everywhere somehow to fill into the Square. In threes and fours: over the black-and-white checkered linoleum, at the corners of the roulette table, chasing each other with slender canes; barefoot, wearing their crested blazers, their white Irish cable-knit sweaters with big turtle-neck collars. The red-and-green-and-plaid yellow-haired tinker's child, the boy in shorts; the boy in a girl's coat; the hundreds of children at the second-story windows, where grownups stood and leaned out for the Crowning. The boy in a green coat who sang "Que Sera, Sera." The boy with enormous eyes, the hunchback child, the little shy Houlihan child (the daughter of the contractor); the one who pulled my scarf on Sunday.

Many children at the Nolans' windows. The boy in yellow standing at the yellow window, and the red-headed boy in blue. The tinker girl in a white-velvet and gold Victorian jacket, the one ahead of the pipers. The boy standing lost in happiness beside his tinker father, whose great hand stayed on the boy's thick hair, in tenderness. Children running continually up to the center of the Square, around and under the blue posts of the tower, putting their hands around the flimsy posts and swinging themselves past under the white goat. The children with the party hats, green paper, gold, white, bright pink, lavender and gold.

The young Green Queen running among the children, playing over the paper streamers, running diagonally over a black-and-white checkerboard.

Now very slowly and imprecisely, a slow and slapstick dumbshow. We watch two men in shirtsleeves, one with a hammer, begin in slow motion, a reversed and unattended ceremony. Slowly, one hammers. Grumbling and gossiping, he hammers his thumb, stops and discusses its effect on European trends: halts; sucks the thumb and one or two fingers; resumes, with a little hopping dance. Very slowly, with imperceptible steps of development, the two men are able to do something to the pulley system. One of the men climbs a ladder which is again set against the tower.

He is on the second story, and he calls up something inaudible to the goat. The answer comes, in a long ragged pennant of scent of goat. A third man appears, carrying a long ladder horizontally. He swings it as he approaches, and the sign that says AFTONS is groaning; it is ripped away from its standard. It clatters to the ground. For a long moment, the other two men stop and look at the sign. By now, the third man has propped his ladder on the second story slowly, with a wobbling progress, he climbs to the goat's throne and attaches a hook to the roof of the platform.

The contractor materializes on the lowest story of the tower, and makes the oration of the Lowering. It soon ends—"... set free in his mountain home in McGillycuddy's Reeks..."

The goat is lowered. They take off his crown, put the ex-king into a small van that is waiting at the foot of the tower, throw the crown in after him, and drive away down the hill. The men with their hammers and claws are at the corner posts. The flags of the Kingdom of Ireland are coming down. The tower is already beginning to be dismantled.

A woman behind me says, in an American accent—flat, Midwestern (Indiana?), hysterical—"What do they do with him? Do they kill him?"

"Could we go and see what happens?" I ask Nicholas.

"I wouldn't miss it," he says under his breath.

There is a moment of deep silence. Somebody says, "I know—donkey race first, then they'll take him away. See you next Puck!"

There is time to go to the Post Office. It is just about to close, but I want to mail my notebook to Paul Rotha. That is all I want to do. Let a film crew not come here.

An old man is buying a stamp, the stamp that has the painting on the glue side, at the Inn. The rocks and islands. I wait for him to lick it and fix it to his letter. Then I say to the postmaster: "Do you have a large manila envelope?"

He looks at me with a fixed stare.

"O God no!" he says.

13

AT THE foot of the hill, the donkey race has not yet begun. Something powerful and unknown is holding it up. And the children, who they said would not take over, have taken over completely. Their running, their games, their light-color darting occupations, fill and color this hill. The donkeys wait.

Then, from the river road, past the miles of caravans, from the direction of Killarney, it begins. Until it is over, no donkey race, no matter how important, no freeing of the king, can start.

It is the funeral of Mrs. McGillycuddy, some relative of the mountains, clearly. Who, after a full life, as a very old woman, broke her hip, died, and is traveling to the burial ground. The streets are lined with Puck Fair people, waiting for the Donkey Derby, with ninety pounds as a prize, and a great many bets riding the favorite, whose name is Sputnik.

The Donkey Derby waits. The funeral procession has entered upon the Laune Bridge, and is climbing the hill. Standers at the edges of the route—and race course—cross themselves. Sadness and black advance; the first few cars, with the closest relatives, pass. The cars go by, eleven, fifteen. By the seventeenth car, the procession and the streets still carry sadness. Twenty-five, thirty-three. By the thirty-seventh car, the majesty of a full grand procession is beginning to assert itself over the grief. Forty-six, fifty-nine, seventy-one.

By the eighty-seventh car, we have a lighted, radiant holiday; a monster picnic winding all along the Killarney road. It would take over Killorglin, if anything but the children could.

And even the children, for two minutes more, hold back. We are waiting with a few of them at the shed where the goat in his van holds back. Now the donkeys hurtle up the hill, racing from the Laune Bridge through the Square to Tobin's Corner, with Sputnik, the favorite, well in the lead even at the beginning. As they charge up the hill, the van's engine roars, is thrown into gear, and goat in his van plunges across the road and along the Glencar road, with us behind him, his only followers.

Up the road toward the Reeks—the road I know well today, past men driving Kerry cattle and holding sun in the distance. The turf lies cut but not gathered in this wet August. The green small truck diminishes before us. Now it slows down, with a knot of people gathered in the road. Around something, in dread.

We come up to the scene in the road. Five or six men are gathered around a fallen man in the middle of the way—the young drover who had come into the fight with O'Connor that first night, after the leaping triumph of the Spanish sailor. We do not stop, for the green van moves on, but in that held moment, I see the lying-down man, flung down as if from a height and surely dead; the mistreated vicious horse held by four men, frothing, trembling, his quarters twitching. And O'Connor with his hands before his face, and two men guarding him. He takes his hands away, and I see in a glimpse the flaming and bloody face, broken-nosed, with a great wet horseshoe mark across the forehead and cheek. What steps in what gasping fight of these three—man, man, and horse—took us here, I do not know. But we are here, and here are the signs.

The goat in the van ahead gains speed again. I see his horns silhouetted against the grating. In the early evening, every now and then, a strong familiar trail of smell.

Along the road, to a sharp turning under trees. To the goat farm? Yes.

We stop behind the stopped van, and talk to people we have seen as we drove past other times. The old woman in a green shawl. The old man, his long rake a fine instrument. The three smiling shy grandchildren. Great-grandchildren?

Then Nicholas, as the door of the van is opened, "Now he will go to join his wives."

But the Puck, set on his hoofs on the ground, the cord at last cut away from his horns, steps, steps, over the stream of the ditch beside the road, in majesty and repose. No need to break through, nothing in reaction, nothing that they said.

White against the hill, cropping, solitary.

Above him, far up the hill, white, scattered, the white herd.

14

WE SAID our good-byes in the doorway of the Inn. Chris and Nicholas packed every centimeter of the car, and Katy Evans and Liadain shook hands. Liadain, her box of colors and brushes in hand, got into the back seat.

Katy said to me, "Here then," and "Come back soon," and threw her arms about me, and gave me two glasses of the Waterford I had seen as water itself halted, and shadow, in glass. I'll send you the earrings from Lord & Taylor one day, I thought, and kissed her good-bye. The room, the dreams, the turf fire in silence.

She looked into my face, and something was drawn behind her look of closeness. "Go easy on Puck," she said, and we drove to Valentia.

Rain is painting the stones of the dock; but across the channel, the sun falls butter-yellow on the Royal, that will be home tonight for us. And in the channel, among whitecaps, two new Spanish trawlers. The rain that stops at once. Evening sun with a white light on the boats and the coast and the quay, the hills dark, the water darker, but the whitecaps and the white rowboat very white and the light-blue fishing boat in again and bright, on the other side of the stones. Shell Oil drums, a large crate stenciled INDIA but full of bread, most likely from Cahirciveen.

A curious subsiding feeling in the car, with the ferry far out in the channel, going very slowly. It is carrying a coffin across the water, and on the far side a small procession comes in the telescope clear light to the water's edge: a priest in black with a broad white ribbon diagonally from his shoulder, on which rests the white rosette. The seven people with him, the horse and cart waiting behind them to receive the coffin.

We get out. A woman on the dock turns to me. "It's the lad of the motorbike accident. In Putney," she says. The ferry slowly moves slanting across the current of the channel.

Nicholas walks around the car and kicks the tire. "Damn, it's flat," he says, and looks around. Leaning against the shed, the customs inspector who deals with the Spanish boats is watching; and, above our heads, two men are sitting on the steep roof of a house—a slate roof, half-finished. They are sitting up there and smoking. With the utmost deliberation, with slow nods to the inspector, as Nicholas stands studying the wheel as if at any moment he might discover the formula to solve its weakness—the three men, in slow motion, converge on the car. One of the roofers and the inspector stand behind the car. They nod to the other roofer, and they take the maroon car in their hands and lift the rear end in the air. Higher than a jack could prop it. And the other roofer changes the tire, and tightens all the bolts, clapping the hub-cap to, just as the ferry comes in.

Nicholas is giving them something. The inspector will take nothing; but the roofers accept with half-smiles, gravely really, and one after the other climb their tall ladder to the slates as we board the ferry. At the last moment, Bill Higgins jumps on. He keeps glancing at Liadain.

The sitting gulls. Three gulls flying; one going backward in the strong wind, for a moment not moving at all, and then in a long curve, outwitting all the prevailing forces.

Owen Cross is in the doorway. I had phoned him from the Inn; or rather, Katy Evans had called him and made reservations for two more rooms, and I had said a word. "Three friends," he says now, in his brown-and-black, hawk-nosed way, "instead of one rich American wife; that may be better, after all."

Dinner is really past; only the later diners are in the room, sitting over coffee. When the door opens, a lovely sound rushes around the corner from the bar. Seamus Coleman beams at me in greeting; he has beautiful lavender strokes under his eyes, he has been at Puck. I want my friends to see his paintings, for this boy from Tullamore who works summers as porter at the Royal is a real one. This is a painter who is a boy who is a porter; and we look at the piercing black, the roofs of the distilleries, the slope and stacks, the shadow black that finally clears and lets you see houses under their walls: Irish, recognizable anywhere, with narrow alleys and one window that at first you do not know is lit.

Out of the window. The green ferry boat far to the left, its color almost lost in night. Foam breaking high on her. A little black dog looks out over the channel. The Spanish boats have come in close; heavy weather tonight, and there is work to do on one of the anchors and its chain. Dark low cloud against almost as dark. Two rusted sisters, out from Vigo. The *Josefa Lopez.*

"They have fine Spanish brandy, cheap," says Bill Higgins behind us as we stand in the road. The sign beside us in the wind can just be read. The hydrangea bushes over the edge make a rushing sound of taffeta. I read Slate Quarry 2½ and know where the roof across the dark channel was dug; Glanleam 1½—that's the Uniackes, and the Knights of Kerry before them; then, on the other side, Chapeltown, Baile an Capal 3, and Tur Brei, Bray Tower 7.

Darkness fills over the words. The lights of the trawlers make their constellations.

Liadain and Bill Higgins are talking. "Care to have a drink?" he asks. "In a little while," she agrees, and sets half an hour from now, and the bar.

We are in the "American" room, past the cool shadowy halls, with the gas-fire turned on. The four of us revolve, revolve; all the encounter, all the changes and withdrawing dance and the comings together very plain as we watch each other now, and speak. But we say nothing at all. Chris is telling of a place where a banshee is known to be, he has heard of it many times, and he swivels around on Nicholas, asking, "Might it not be race-memory?"

"No, it might *not*," in a knot of crossness Nicholas answers; and says to Liadain, "Go ahead and have your drink!"

"I'll do that," says Liadain, and goes to the black hall.

"I'll look at these," Chris says, at the magazines.

We go down the hall to the little library. It is empty; next door, in the games room, the light sound of a ping-pong ball struck in excellent humor.

He begins to speak to me at once, as if the entire time had all been moving here.

All my boy's life was killing, he is saying. Foxes, seafishing, the beaters in the woods. When I think of all the small animals! It was all very exciting. But it was killing.

I hear everything he is saying as if it were emerging from within my own life. How do we come to be talking about the bells slung between the horns of the goat, in the middle of his story? Three bells, he says, the three; it is always the testicles and the penis. I think: but weren't there five bells? I am no longer sure, for it is the face of the goat I see: golden eyes, hieratic beard, long curl of lip where speech arises, intellection, or where speech is no longer necessary since something whole is already being expressed. There were five bells.

We go on with the brandy that is suddenly in my hand. He is among his words... the Austen Chamberlain children, in the nursery with them, and—do you know Sarah Clancharlie?... and Lady Clancharlie, my cousin, he is saying; they wanted me to be in business, or publishing, and I told you, don't you remember, of how I started a job by catching O'Brien—he spoke of you once to me—catching O'Brien, the story man, as he jumped aboard a train at King's Cross. But none of it made sense, he was saying, I wanted to start again.

Lady Clancharlie coming to Dublin, and of course I wanted her to meet Hanaghan. How could I convey to her, to anyone, the quality of that man, what he could do? A consultant job? no, I didn't ask for anything for him, no, surely not; and besides, Lady Clancharlie was *not* impressed....

All they can think of is what I gave up. They said I had married a peasant—Earth, song, our struggle, our unfolding—you know what I married.

Because you are pure, he is saying. I know writing people, theater people, what they want things to be. And because you were pure in all of that—He waved his long arm of bone, the glitter fine in his eye, his leather patches on the elbow very close to me, all part of my life forever—I was drawn to you, I love you, I told Liadain that it should, between us, be a romantic thing, as part of Puck.

I know you, I know you, he is saying to me. I know the sadness, the struggle in you, woman, the struggle still going on, what is accepted and what is not fully accepted. I know what it is, he is saying; and then in harshness and suddenness, a voice breaks through below his voice.

God is your dad, he is saying in a rasping voice, God is your daddy, yes, say it in the familiar way, the way you remember when you ran across the room with your arms up. He is, he needs you as much as you need him. Fight it out, he is saying.

Perhaps this will sound funny in the morning.

I had to speak to you about yourself and about myself.

Body to body first—we could have done that, he is saying, O easily easily we could, but it is dust, he is saying. It is dust. But spirit to spirit—It is man you need, he said, and the spirit of man.

We kiss, it is he that I am kissing and he kisses me, constellating a scene. We are on an enormous pier, the ship so tall behind him that will carry him away, lifting him, lifting him as he kisses me, in love that now belongs to him as I belong to love, carrying him far and forever away in the kiss.

15

IT HAS all come through for me, in the most curious brief endless random moment, the moment and all it contains, with a man speaking to me as a wise and loving and sacred man.

We find Liadain, back again with Chris in the overheated, "American" room. Nicholas keeps my hand tight. He speaks to her in his bantering, married voice: "You did have to go and have a drink with someone you picked up on the ferryboat, didn't you?"

"I did," she answered, looking at me in a long golden smile. "After everything you've had to do with her—and endless pubs, and tinkers, and Morris not seen by me in a lifetime!" She laughed, and kissed me, and said to Nicholas in the same movement, "I like Bill Higgins. He told me a whole story—him and his brother, far ago—postmaster in New London, is there a New London? His brother, now..." She yawned, a high vertical seductive yawn.

"Good night at last," she said, "and good night for the morning, when we leave. Bring your son to visit us in Dublin—our five and your son have to know each other."

She looked at me, and in the brandy light I saw her eyes change, golden look of a goat transformed, look of the poem-goddess, transformed again.

Chris and I were there alone, with a magazine between us.

"He's grand, isn't he, Nicholas?" Chris said. "He's done very much for me, I know, and—well, he won't tell you, and don't let on that I did, but he's Lady Clancharlie's cousin."

He talked to me, in his brown chair, smoke drifting over his pointed eyebrows, his mouth pointed... "I hated what Bryan did to you," he said, glaring at me with a friendly grin, the glare for Bryan. "He could have spoken to you first, and then judged you. I hated it for you."

His words were throwing me back into the press of that moment in Killorglin when he had said, "Bryan won't see you." I had a sharp and acid-colored vision of the Square, the goat above me as I had heard the phrase, the four flags flapping at the corners of the high blue platform, in their own four shadows and colors, lit by the colored lights. The goat king standing there, white and archetypal in his Square. Dominant, isolated, tied by the ankles and ruling my fantasy.

The sight shifted within me. The goat alone gave way to Fursey in the air. The saint on the night sky, the gloom and press of the world at night, Ireland spread out, beneath him. He lived in that black air, moving on nothing like a world in its space. Four flames stood there, as he turned his head, in the four corners of his square of night. As he watched them, they flared up and coalesced. A voice said, "RESPICE MUNDUM." What the orgy says: "Look at the world."

...Chris was talking about Dublin. "Perverse! I told you I was. There's that girl; yes, I've wanted to marry her. But an odd thing happens. I rush up the street, loving her. I ring the doorbell, wanting her, our life, to be in bed with her *now*. Footsteps in the hall, and the door opens. I'm not in her, I'm stepping over the threshold, it all gives way. But once I'm out of the house, I'm there again.... What is she to me? Death? I change in doorways, into my opposite.... It's not like that now, with you."

He went on talking as if he had not heard himself. I stayed very still. "I tell you what I know tonight," he said, and looked at me from under his pointed eyebrows. Suddenly he was possessed of himself, in a way I had not seen him since we met in the Inn at Glenbeigh. Sharp-pointed, superhuman in quickness, keenness; insolent and right. "To come to an orgy!" he said, in a yelping voice. "Alone, and find each other."

The orgy is experience, I thought. The sacred feast.

"The orgy is the meeting," he said, in answer to my thought. His voice took on another note; deep now, and strong. "I know where that cry came from, the cry the Greek sailor heard. The voice that called from the island, 'Pan is dead'—You know whose voice that was?"

His question called me back. "No. Whose voice?" Winds, worshipers?

"Whose voice does it have to be? It is Pan's own voice. I hear the animal shout, and the god's laugh in the overtone."

Owen puts his head around the door, and the moment cracks. "Ah!" he barks sharply. "Muriel! Just a word, an invitation for tomorrow dinner. My friends the Uniackes—that's Glanleam, the great place where the Knights of Kerry lived, with its rhododendron and tropical garden and bim-bam-boo—the Uniackes want you and me to come to drinks tomorrow, and then we'll all have dinner here. And Colonel Uniacke says to tell you he's heard you want facts about Puck Fair. He told me he'll send you to somebody who'll give you facts. They may not be true, he says, but they'll be facts."

The moment had turned. Even though, later, Chris asked me, "But why couldn't it be between *us*... but we both are lonely... but we both are afraid, aren't we?" It was the crossed pass, the kind of invitation Dylan Thomas used to make. I was still.

I said good night to him at my room door. I went into the little room. Alone, I thought. The tension between the aloneness and the giant press of the crowd. Isolation, orgy, and the single creature held in a square, a diagram of the world. In the texture of reality. Until it is reconciled and made relation, made marriage. Until I know the opposite and the other side of the moment, what we are kept in ignorance of. What I keep myself in ignorance of.

And none of this is possible to say. How could I ever say it to anyone? What is it saying to me?

Look at the world again.

I would stay here. I would not go to Dublin, and find writers, and try to promote a movie. I did not care—I would rather a film crew never came to this town, or set its actors here and there, gleaming, false. I would rather the tourists never touched Killorglin.

As for myself. There had been a revelation. Of what? I began to know; and I saw how the temptation was to go back to the moment *before* revelation, to go on with one's old life. I thought of my son. All that quickness, that transforms and comes through.

I thought of person after person who had risen up for me here. No, that is before, I thought. Jonah is before; I start from here.

My friend who sent me here; she is real: her gift is here, in this room and in me tonight. I began a letter to her:

> *Mixed... in a tragic, penetrating beauty, music and filth, cattle and drunkenness, the gypsies the goat & the marvelous children. It had a heavy dark beauty, a misery too, and all the time the implication of some bright release. It came, but in ways that were not part of the design. Everything one heard was true, and then heard was not true,* was *indeed there and true—but in a different way.*
>
> *Otherwise, as you say.*

I would stay here, and go on from here. I would go to the Skelligs in a day of sun and strong suction against the rock, and climb those tottering rock steps. The gannets cry, the lighthouse keepers stick to the radio, for news of the air disaster that they heard all night. The airliner shattered, just out of Cork, over the sea; the man at the radio who could not get the name of the boy found with one arm in his life preserver. "David—David—like the young queen of England's little lad—"

The tight stonemasonry of the beehive cells, in the flowery height, with the foam a thousand feet below one's knees. Climb of penance on the wet stones. This I would do, and go these roads, and try to avoid everything I might interpose between myself and what was in me, what I was in. No myth, no mask, no legendary figure. And what of that last rainy afternoon, thinking already of Shannon, the plane, and my young son flying to meet me in New York—when hailing me on the road came the actual woman of the roads. Then I had left Valentia in a driving storm, the disaster signal going crump! and compressing the whole air with its implosion, rain on the roads, a sheep fair in Killorglin, and on the wet road, Katy Sullivan for whom I stopped in my rented car, to be delivered at Shannon as I boarded my plane.

Katy Sullivan, four teeth, shingled, no, crew-cut, patched, botched in rags and linings, padded, begging me, "Take me on the plane with you! Hide me, and take me to America!" God, how can any of it be met? She meets it: she is going to do the Stations of the Cross for me tonight.

But now it is now, and I look out the window. The Spanish sailors are out there, and they will be, when I come home from the Skelligs tomorrow. Eating live shrimp, with the legs hanging from their mouths in whiskers, and smiling, and the Irish girls crazy to *bailar* with them once more before they sail. They will go to the movies that Owen Cross shows every other Saturday night, go to the *baile* and then out as soon as Sunday gets sea-legs, into the deeper Atlantic mist. The clarity.

Sound of coughing outside. A song in the black, a ballad going "You promised me..." and then an "O" prolonged, perpetual regret. Coughing. Footsteps.

No, I cannot stay here, I cannot finish that letter, restlessness possesses me beyond any lovely theoretical question of proceeding from revelation. And how will I, anyway? What is it? Something like the fisherman doing his long endless casts over the Laune, a river that is before one, and the endless attempt at art, or life? How do I do it?

I would like to go downstairs and find somebody.

Slight sounds coming from the bar.

Owen Cross there, and the brave-faced, slender woman who runs the hotel with him, tending bar, and Bill Higgins alone on the end stool.

"You're just in time," the woman says, and gives me a drink, "Owen's begun to tell us of the virtues of the proposed bridge to Valentia Island."

"Proposed!" he cries. "It's practically a reality. It's been voted in, hasn't it?"

"Owen!" I said, and sat on the stool in the middle. "Do it the—how shall I say?—the American way. Wish for it clear of rain and cold, no sheep, no petrol drums—wish for an air-conditioned tunnel."

They laughed, and the girl and Owen bent their heads close over the bar.

The radio behind the bar stopped its music. Pause. Then a new voice cut in, above static.

"Irish Freedom Radio comes back on the air... after a silence of several months." We listened hard; there were sounds of scratching, of pushing, but the voice came through.

"This is the voice of the I.R.A.," it said, "broadcasting from occupied Ireland. We make this announcement so that our listeners may know that we now expect to come on the air at regular intervals.

"Long live the Republic."

And then, through the broken waves and pulses of sound, the scratching, the deep-sea moan, struggled out of the bar radio the recorded music of "The Mountains of Pomeroy."

An outlawed man in a land forlorn,
He scorned to turn and fly,
But kept the cause of freedom safe
Upon the mountains high.

The record ended; only the scratching sound was left; then air silence. Hardly anything was said. Owen and the girl drank; he, Guinness; she, Baby Cham.

But Bill Higgins wanted, now, to talk. He moved to the stool beside me. "I'm glad you came in," he said. "I liked talking to Mrs. Hilliard. And I'm nowhere near finished. I want to speak—not Kerry, not Dublin, not New London—but the whole other side of the world. The side that may be as far from us—but it isn't, it's only opposite. Just there. At hand.

"I sailed those seas and rivers, you know," he said. "It's all very fine—San Francisco, Paris, New York. Ah but the East, that's what you want to see. That's a whole new world. The four sights—you know what they are? The blue hills behind Sydney, that beach of New Zealand, what's its name? And then there's Peking.

"But the best is the gorge—the bends of the Yangtze Kiang. There's a man at that bend that's a happy man. He has a box at his back: you'd say a kennel. He sits with his line. He sits. He catches his fish." Bill Higgins laid one hand, its edge, hard on the palm of the other. "He splits his fish. He cleans it. He adds his bit of curry and rice and cooks them and eats them, and goes into his box again. He's happy.

"There was one man we saw in Peking. Shipwrecked, he was, in the South Atlantic; for three months he was alone on a raft, and he lived. Naked; without food or drink; without anything. No help anywhere. The flying-fish came by in the air, sometimes beside him, but sometimes they flew right over his square raft. At first he couldn't get his hand on them; but then, later, he could, they said. I saw him there, as close as I am to you. He reached up his hand right into the air; he caught them, he lived off of them. Patience. And skill. Alone on that floating square. Around the earth from here. And then plunged into the crowd in Peking. An endless crowd it was.

"Alone and naked he floated.

"It's a whole new world."

THE BALLS OF THE GOAT

Torrent that rushes down
Knocknadober,
Make the channel deeper
Where I ferry home;

Winds go west over
Left Handed Reaper,
Mountain that gathered me
Out of my old shame—

Your white beard streaming,
Puck of summertime,
At last gave me
My woman's name.

ACKNOWLEDGMENTS

1965

MY GRATEFUL acknowledgment to Jonathan Hanaghan for granting me permission to quote from his *Society, Evolution & Revelation*. The Runa Press, Monkstown, Dublin. To the Macmillan Company for lines from "The Stolen Child," in *Collected Poems* by W. B. Yeats. To Random House, Inc., for "In West Kerry" by John M. Synge. Copyright 1935 by the Modern Library, Inc. Reprinted from *The Complete Works* of John M. Synge. To Faber and Faber Ltd. for "The Horned God," by Margaret Murray in *The God of the Witches*. To Tony Inglis for the story on page 74.

1997

GRATEFUL acknowledgment is made to Frank Music Corp., for permission to quote from "A Woman in Love," by Frank Loesser, copyright © 1955 (Renewed) by Frank Music Corp. All rights reserved. To Beechwood Music Corp., for permission to quote from "Big Man," by Glen Larson and Bruce Belland, copyright © 1958 Beechwood Music Corp., Copyright Renewed 1986 Beechwood Music Corp. All rights reserved. International copyright secured. Used by permission. To Jay Livingston Music and St. Angelo Music, for permission to quote from "Que Sera Sera (Whatever Will Be, Will Be)," by Jay Livingston and Ray Evans, copyright © 1985 (Renewed) by Jay Livingston and Ray Evans and assigned to Jay Livingston Music and St. Angelo Music. All rights reserved. Used by permission. To Dick Cameron and The Runa Press, Dublin, for the use of excerpts from *Society, Evolution & Revelation*, by Jonathan Hanaghan. All rights reserved. Reprinted by permission of Dick Cameron and The Runa Press.

ABOUT MURIEL RUKEYSER

THE LEGACY of Muriel Rukeyser (1913-1980) is one of controversy and commitment, iconoclasm and optimism, compassion and social criticism. With an unequaled breadth of knowledge and depth of emotional insight, Rukeyser extended the boundaries of American literature. She wrote about subjects as diverse as biology and architecture, anthropology and physics, psychology and religion. She broke through the taboos of her time, writing candidly about sexuality, motherhood, the female body, lesbian love, eroticism. She saw poetry as the very essence of our everyday lives—inseparable from politics, from science, from religious belief, from sexuality, from human community.

Throughout her career, Rukeyser eschewed safety and detachment in favor of passionate involvement with society and current events. Rukeyser's capacious approach to her life and work did not come without cost, however, and her history illustrates the penalties that can be assessed against creative individuals whose compassion and allegiances cross many boundaries and refuse a limited definition. She polarized critical opinion with her radical social convictions and her actions, taken on behalf of humanitarian issues that concerned her—among them women's rights, anti-Semitism, civil rights, environmentalism, and the antiwar movement. Often censured and misunderstood for her various involvements, she never, in her lifetime, received the full recognition she deserved. The poet Kenneth Rexroth once observed that there may never have been an American poet who deserved the Nobel Prize as much as Muriel Rukeyser did.

Yet, this is not to suggest that Rukeyser did not hold powerful positions during her lifetime. She taught at the California Labor School, Vassar College, Columbia University, and Sarah Lawrence College, playing a pivotal role in the development of such writers as Alice Walker, for whom she served as a mentor. She was a member of the Academy of Arts and Letters, and she served as president of P.E.N. American Center. Nor did her writings go unrecognized during her lifetime. Her first collection of poems, *Theory of Flight*, written when she was a college student, won the prestigious Yale Younger Poets Prize in 1935. Among her other "toys of fame" were the Copernicus Award, the Shelley Memorial Award, and Guggenheim Awards.

Muriel Rukeyser lived most of her life in New York City and was educated at Vassar and Columbia. In addition to fifteen collections of poetry, Rukeyser published plays, children's fiction, translations of Octavio Paz, Gunnar Ekelöf, Bertolt Brecht, and biographies of Wendell Willkie, Thomas Hariot, and the physicist Willard Gibbs. She also wrote the essential exploration of American culture, *The Life of Poetry*—an extended essay that sets forth her all-embracing philosophy of the central role of poetry in a democratic society.

BOOKS BY MURIEL RUKEYSER

PROSE

The Life of Poetry

The Traces of Thomas Hariot

Houdini (Play)

The Colors of the Day (Play)

One Life

The Middle of the Air (Play)

Willard Gibbs

POETRY

The Collected Poems of Muriel Rukeyser

The Gates

Breaking Open

29 Poems

The Speed of Darkness

The Outer Banks

Waterlily Fire: Poems 1935-1962

Body of Waking

Selected Poems

Elegies

Orpheus

The Green Wave

Beast in View

The Soul and Body of John Brown

A Turning Wind

U.S. 1

Theory of Flight